Eddie Bazil

SOUND
EQUALIZATION
TIPS AND TRICKS

PC Publishing

PC Publishing
Keeper's House
Merton
Thetford
Norfolk IP25 6QH
UK

Tel +44 (0)1953 889900
email info@pc-publishing.com
website http://www.pc-publishing.com

First published 2009

ISBN 13: 978 1906005 092

British Library Cataloguing in Publication Data
A catalogue record for this book is available from the British Library

Printed and bound in Great Britain by The Cromwell Press Group, Trowbridge, Wilts

Contents

Introduction to EQ

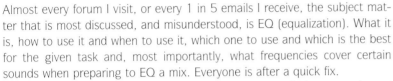

Almost every forum I visit, or every 1 in 5 emails I receive, the subject matter that is most discussed, and misunderstood, is EQ (equalization). What it is, how to use it and when to use it, which one to use and which is the best for the given task and, most importantly, what frequencies cover certain sounds when preparing to EQ a mix. Everyone is after a quick fix.

To define what equalization is would take quite a while but a condensed definition would be:

- A dynamic process which uses filters to alter the balance of frequencies in a sound. This is achieved by using a number of filter circuits which apply positive or negative gain to selected frequency ranges. The positive gain is referred to as 'boost' and the negative gain is referred to as 'cut'.

This is as simple as you can get. In fact, this definition has helped me considerably and particularly when I was a beginner.

Sadly, today's 'new' mentality is to download as many plug-ins as possible and let the presets do all the work. The problem with this approach is that presets are not only guides but serve no real purpose when it comes to actual examples of dynamic processing of real life examples. We have also arrived into the preset based EQ world for most hi-fi owners. In fact, this has got to the point whereby hi-fi manufacturers put preset EQ settings on their systems for the listener to choose from. Ghastly presets called Pop, Ambient, Disco etc are predefined EQ templates that you can tweak to your heart's content. This thinking has now crossed over to the world of vsts. Whereas, presets can be of limited use in putting the process in a ball park, I think they do more damage than good.

Additionally, because most beginners have not had a proper grounding or education in the technical aspects of mixing, we all had to start somewhere, they are left in the abyss of 'confused knowledge'. No understanding or taking the time to learn what dynamics are and how they function is the equivalent of sitting in an automatic car and expecting to be driving simply by switching it on and putting it into gear.

And, there is some extremely poor advice floating around on badly informed websites regarding the whole mixing process and particularly when it comes to using dynamics and effects. The worst of these is that of using EQ and compression on just about every sound in the mix and in multi instances (running three compressors and two EQs on a single channel/sound).

I am not quite sure which idiot came out with this nugget, but it primarily originated in the Hip Hop and Dance genres whereby compression and EQ can be used to dynamically add extra colour to a sound. I am not against this thinking but am against the overuse of any dynamic or effect. However, using EQ and compression not only on every sound but many instances of it defies all the sense that we teach to engineers.

Think about this in simple sensible terms: why take a sound and reshape it so many times that it doesn't sound like the original sound any more? On top of that, what beginners (and some pros unfortunately) do not seem to realise is that adding many instances of dynamic processing, one on top of the other, degrades the sound and compromises its sonic integrity.

Good mixing engineers work around this problem the proper way, i.e. start with a sound already close to the sound they want to attain and then tweak it to taste. EQ is a wonderful tool, used to shape and accent a sound, not to be used as a mauling tool that some regard as a prerequisite to the start of any mix process.

• EQ is one of the most powerful tools available to a producer and mastering engineer, and to master this tool one needs to understand frequencies.

In the mix/production areas, understanding frequencies is the most fundamental part of manipulating sound. Without understanding the basic concepts of sound and how it travels, how can you truthfully begin to understand how to use the dynamics that are needed to process the sound?

When the term 'EQ' (equalization) is mentioned, people invariably think of the tone controls on their hi-fi systems. Knowing this actually gives you a head start. The fact that a sound can be made 'warmer' or 'punchier' already gives you an idea as to what EQ is. You know that by turning the treble knob up on your hi-fi makes the sound brighter, turning it down makes the sound less bright and more fluffy or woollen.

When you turn the knob 'up' you are 'boosting the predetermined frequencies that are assigned to that knob'. When you turn the knob 'down' you are cutting those frequencies.

Before we get deep into EQ, let us look back a tad at why EQ was introduced into our lives in the first place.

How and why

This whole headache began in the broadcasting field. Blame those guys. Hell, I always do. Actually the first ever instances of equalization was in the communications industry. EQ was used to counteract some of the problems in telephone systems. It then transgressed into the broadcasting industry.

Tone controls were created and used to compensate technical inaccuracies in the recording chain, more notably, compensating for microphone colouration and room acoustics. EQ was used as a means of controlling the gain of a range of frequencies.

This form of equalization is termed 'corrective or compensatory' EQ and is still used today to compensate for poor room acoustics, or rooms with an acoustical/frequency bias. It can act as a half measure stop gap for monitoring in a truer sense (i.e. what goes in and what comes out).

In those early days standard 'bass, middle and treble' gain controls were all we had. Today, we are actually spoilt for choice as there are so many parameters that we can control on any type of EQ, that it has actually become quite confusing for beginners and even experienced users. Not only are there more parameters to contend with, but there is also 'new' terminology to contend with.

The object of this book is to make the subject of EQ as clear to understand as possible using both text, images and audio examples. Theory helps a great deal but with a strong grounding in the simple technicalities of EQ and with enough hands-on experience one can get a good idea of how to use EQ without having a physics degree.

This entire book can be split into two distinct themes: Corrective and Creative Equalization. Let me briefly explain what each one is.

Corrective equalization

Corrective equalization is used to correct any anomalies that may exist in a sound (removing noise, rumble etc, and abating problematic frequencies, compensating for room inaccuracies etc). However, precision EQ tasks will require corrective methods as opposed to creative ones.

A good example of this would be to use corrective EQ to separate frequencies in a mix. Corrective EQ is also used at the mastering stage to compensate and accommodate frequencies that would otherwise render the master as 'unacceptable'.

In other words the mastering engineer will use corrective EQ to create a master suitable for the desired medium. Of course, creative EQ techniques also play a part, but first and foremost the master must be as 'correct' as possible with consideration for the entire frequency spectrum of the master.

Creative equalization

Creative equalization is used to 'colour' a sound, or to reshape its characteristics to create a new sonic template (boosting the mid-range frequencies of a kick drum to accent the punch and body is a good example).

It is also used in a wider context to manipulate a range of frequencies, such as in a mix, to attain a new 'colour'. A good example of this would be to use EQ to make a mix more dynamic at the lower and higher frequencies in the event that the mix is geared for the club scenes. In many cases a good hardware EQ can act as a medium to 'warm' sound in a way that software based EQs cannot, although today they are closing that gap considerably. We will touch on this later as the subject of hardware versus software seems to be a thorny subject discussed at length by engineers and mastering engineers alike.

- From corrective EQ we have come a long way to creative EQ.

Tip

Check my website http://www.samplecraze.com for coverage of the subject of sound in detail.

The natural progression from a 'corrective' tool to a 'creative' one is not uncommon in the technological world and none more so than the audio and communications industries. We seem to share a great deal with each other. I do not want to bore you with the history of EQ or who invented what. You can trawl the internet for some excellent articles on this subject. What I want to do is to dive in and get you started on this detailed and confusing subject.

However, before I get into this deeper, I need you to understand 'sound' and 'frequencies'. Those that have read my tutorials on my website http://www.samplecraze.com will know that I have covered the subject of sound in detail. I will include a condensed version very shortly.

I would also like to point out that the audio editor of choice used in this book is Sound Forge. You can of course migrate and apply all the ensuing techniques to an audio editor of your choosing. But I have always worked with Sound Forge and like its user interface, utilities and functionality.

Tagging

To fully benefit from the information supplied in this book I suggest the following technique/method. It is one that I have used for most of my life and one that I feel works extremely well when I tutor students. It is of course up to you if you want to adopt this technique, but at the very least I hope you will give it a chance. Who knows, you might find it helpful in other areas of your life!

The technique is called Tagging and it will help you to understand the terminology and definitions (and what each part is and does). It is a system that has existed for centuries and works extremely well in every aspect of your life.

It is a system that speed reading specialists, memory recall centres and even high powered executive training programs use. It is the simplest and most effective 'remembering' tool.

You have used it since you were a child. Every time you were asked to draw a house in a field, you would draw a strong big house on green grass with a huge sun that was always yellow, red or orange with a tree and a cow. Of course some people drew the same topic in the Picasso mould or surreal a la Dali, but on the whole, the picture is almost always the same.

Why? Because we remember things that have an effect on our senses, be it touch, smell, taste, hearing or visual. The strong colour of the sun and the size of it are a great way of remembering what a sun looks like. The big house in the centre of the drawing will always stay in your mind. The cow is always alone and strongly accentuated and is always totally out of size in comparison to the house. The ground is always green grass and the sky always blue and if there is a cloud then it is always one big round cloud.

These images are strong and always stay in memory. The same technique is used in tagging. We create an image rich in as many of the senses as possible and that will always stay in our minds, far stronger than having to learn things in parrot fashion.

I have used this technique all my life and now do it unconsciously. Not only does it work but it is also fun as the tool for tagging is your imagination and nothing is stronger or stays longer in your memory than an image created out of your imagination.

Probably by now you feel that I require a great deal of help and that there are certain places for people like me, comfortable places that offer 24 hour security and in depth treatment. You are probably right - but try it.

I use colour to understand and shape sound. I break sound down into its coloured counterparts. The decision as to what colour represents which frequency spread is down to you. I use the colour blue for precision and correction and the colour red for creative and additive. In terms of texture I use blue for cold and red for warmth. Between these two colours lie all the varying qualities of sound.

When I mix a song I think in colours and try to achieve a varied and sustained palette of colours that define the mix in terms of accuracy/definition and overall 'feel'.

I find that the more ways you find to tag a piece of information the more chance there is of you remembering and recalling that information. Apart from colour and sound I use humour and find it to be very effective.

You will always remember the person who slipped on a banana and fell down that morning when running for a bus you were waiting for. But will you remember the other people in the queue with you?

The more impact the image carries the more chance of the 'tag' being ingrained into your memory.

Once you have 'tagged' colours/images to sound you are then afforded an additional form of reference that will aid you greatly in defining frequencies and how to manipulate them. Think of this as an additional 'sense'; one that is used to further help the aural side of understanding sound. I have been using this method for years and find it to be invaluable.

Everyone has their own system I am sure, and whatever works for you should be used. I wanted to share this method simply because, for me, it works really well. Music is about massaging the senses. The more senses we can use the more pronounced our memory recall will be.

So, let us begin this journey.

What is sound?

If there is one chapter of this book that you must fully understand, this is it. Don't skip over it. Don't make excuses about knowing it all already. Read it all!

To understand any part of EQ you need to understand sound; what it is, how it moves, how we perceive it and why we perceive it the way we do. Once you understand this then shaping it or manipulating it becomes so much easier.

- Sound is the displacement of air around the source and how we perceive that displacement.

Right, what does that mean?
Think of the best and most commonly used analogy: that of dropping a stone in a pond and watching the ripples form. The ripples always move away from where the stone meets the water (source). The 'air displacement' is the ripples created by the dropping stone. In this case we see the ripples. In the case of sound we hear the ripples (the displaced air).

How do we hear the displaced air?
Our eardrums pick up the displaced air and our brains then process the data as sound. I could go into the details about the ear muscle vibrating and the eardrum being a chamber and on and on and on … but that is not what this book is about, although it would make for an interesting subject sometime in the future.

What is important to understand is that there is a direct relationship between sound in the space it occupies and travels to/from and our interpretation of it. The tagging image here is the ripple.

Has it ever occurred to you that when a picture is drawn of a guitar amplifier, with a guitarist playing loudly, you always see a few arced lines drawn coming out of the amplifier? Exactly like the ripples in the pond. In fact this image is often the same for speakers that are playing music. The picture or tag here is always the same, with arced lines starting as small arcs growing to large arcs away from the speaker. Keep that image in your head and that constitutes sound, or more precisely, sound waves like the ripples.

Figure 2.1 illustrates this. I have deliberately used freehand so it will make you laugh and stay in your memory. The arcs/ripples are sound waves that move away from the source.

Figure 2.1
Sound waves

Components of sound

Now let us look at the components that make up sound. These are frequency, wavelength, period, amplitude, intensity, speed, timbre and direction.

We are only going to concentrate on the three integral ones as they are relevant to this subject and are really quite simple to understand if you apply the ripple analogy. The three are:

• Frequency
• Amplitude
• Timbre

The displacement of air (or air pressure as is more commonly known), creates the waves in Figure 2.1 which are known as sound waves. The rate at which these waves occur is called frequency. So our first component of sound is frequency.

Frequency

This is simply calculated at how many cycles (waves) occur every second. These cycles are repeated so really we only need to look at how many cycles (waves) occur in one second. The result is measured as cycles/second and this unit of frequency is called a Hertz and the abbreviation is Hz.

Using the waves/arcs analogy above think of each wave as a cycle and the amount of waves that are dispersed in one second are calculated as frequency. You cannot get simpler than that ... how many cycles hit you in one second.

Heinrich Hertz was a clever chap who worked with wavelengths and frequency, so we have to thank the man and it seemed only right to name this little calculation after him. I always remember the rent-a–car agency when I think of frequencies and Hertz and it makes me smile every time so remembering that name is easy. This is my personal 'tag' for frequency.

To give you an example of how easy this is consider the following example: If you had 50 cycles hit you in one second then that would be a 50 Hz wave. So it also follows and makes complete sense that if you had 10,000 cycles per second then that would be 10,000 Hz, but, because we don't want to have to write so many zeros every time a thousand appears we use the letter k to denote a thousand.

So, 10,000 Hz is now written as 10 kHz. There is a reason we do this and it's not because we want to look deep and complicated individuals but simply because of all the work that has been carried out on our hearing range in the past. We even use the letter K to denote thousands when it comes to money.

'What did you earn last year?' ... '10 K man.'

And a range was formed; sure it varies but generally speaking, our hearing range lies anywhere between 20 Hz (low), to 20 kHz (high).

Now, let us think of that range and make life a lot easier by giving names you recognise to the frequency range. So: bass, midrange and treble are easy to remember and if you are old enough then that's about all that used to exist on hi-fi systems back in the days of armour and jousting. Now let us give those tags a frequency range and then all becomes so much easier to understand. These ranges are not bible but are useful for general referencing.

Bass

10 Hz to 200 Hz. Also known as 'low-end'. Below approximately 10 Hz lies the 'feel' as sound is felt as opposed to heard.

Although it was, and still is to a certain degree, common practice to remove frequencies below 40 Hz when producing a mix this is more for low energy that can 'tire' the listener and make them feel a little ill to the stomach.

Listen to the following two audio files. One is at 10 Hz and the other is at 30 Hz. Although you can, or think you can, 'hear' the 10 Hz file, it is more felt than heard.

What is interesting here, and a point to note, is that both waveforms are exactly the same length (0.10 seconds) and yet there are more cycles for the 30 Hz waveform than the 10 Hz waveform.

Looking at Figures 2.2 and 2.3, you might be thinking to yourself: 'how come there is only one cycle visible for the 10 Hz waveform and three cycles for the 30 Hz waveform?' Normally you would expect to see 10 cycles for the 10 Hz waveform (10 cycles/second) and 30 cycles for the 30 Hz waveform (30 cycles/second). But, because the lengths are 0.10 of a second (1/10 th) then we need to divide by ten. Basically, you are seeing a tenth of the number of cycles that should be visible simply because I have created these two files at a length of a tenth of a second.

Sound files

Listen to the 10 Hz sine wave and then the 30 Hz sine wave

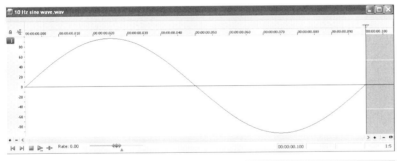

Figure 2.2
10 Hz sine wave

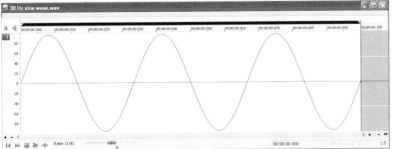

Figure 2.3
30 Hz sine wave

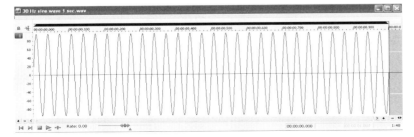

Figure 2.4
30 Hz sine at 1 second length

Had I supplied the full one second diagrams then it could be congested and you would not see the cycles clearly. But for the purists, Figure 2.4 shows the actual 1 second version of the 30 Hz file. Trust me, and if you are in the mood to count, there are thirty (30) cycles in that diagram.

Hopefully this makes the subject of frequency/cycles/time far clearer.

Midrange or mid

A term you hear a lot of engineers use: 200 Hz to about 3 kHz. Also known as 'high low' or 'low high' although rarely referred to as such.

Treble

3 kHz to whatever the highest value you can hear. Also known as 'top-end' and 'high-end'. Above 14 kHz lies the 'air' region, also known as 'space', 'presence' and 'sparkle'. Nicely descriptive for tagging purposes, this range deals with the very bright, or high frequency, ranges and can also be felt as opposed to heard – much like the low-end.

The above are extremely general but will hopefully provide a ball park guide as to the three distinct hi-fi frequency ranges. Of course nowadays we have lots of very descriptive words defining specific ranges. However, the real importance of these basic ranges is to attune your thinking into understanding some of the terminology used when engineering a mix.

These ranges are often further defined with wonderful terms like 'boxy', 'nasal', 'presence', 'woolly' and so on. Understand the approximate frequency ranges and how they are described by engineers and you are halfway there in understanding how to then manipulate these ranges.

Possibly the most important piece of advice I can give in terms of frequency ranges is to always be proactive in listening to well produced and mastered material and then attuning both your ears and brain to understanding the frequencies used and treated in a mix content.

- Try to listen then gauge, listen then gauge. Then tag and tag again.

If you feel the need then by all means use spectrum/frequency analysers to ascertain the frequency content of a sound or mix. Once you get to embed the varying frequency ranges of sounds in your brain (both in a mix context and in isolation) and then reference the values against your hearing, you will be in a strong position to recognise frequency ranges and how to treat them.

At this stage it is important to mention my beliefs regarding frequency charts. I am not talking about the midi number/cycles chart coming up in this tutorial, but about charts depicting ranges of instrument frequencies.

I put very little importance on frequency charts for instruments. Almost every website you visit that displays a frequency chart you will see that they all vary in their ranges. The reason for this is quite simple. Ranges can be both inaccurate and broad. I think it is a waste of time displaying charts, because almost every student I have tutored that has tried to use one of these charts has still ended up requesting help on EQ. Quite often an instrument frequency range chart can be more confusing than helpful. Short of defining orchestral instrument frequency charts it is almost impossible to define, and represent accurately, modern sounds used in mixes. Acoustic instruments will have defined ranges in isolation but these ranges will vary in a mix context and therefore not be very helpful.

Of course if you feel that they are helpful then by all means use them. Anything that can help you is an asset and must not be disregarded.

However, I feel it is far more helpful to understand frequencies and sound, than use a chart of this type. The more you analyse sound by listening to music and marrying each sound element with a frequency, the more you will embed the information into your brain until it becomes second nature to 'guess a frequency' and be pretty close.

Once you understand the content of this book, you won't need a chart. You will be in a position to make far more accurate and detailed analysis of the frequencies that are being heard. Your real life examples and ears will be your assets and not some arbitrary frequency chart.

I will of course give examples of certain sound frequency ranges and what happens when you apply certain EQ parameters to them. This is a given and hopefully the process and result will help you in forming a strong understanding of sound and frequencies.

So we now know that higher frequency sounds are higher in pitch as there are more cycles per second, and lower frequency sounds have fewer cycles per second.

Midi

Right now I think it is important to show you a midi/frequency chart for all the notes on a keyboard, and the midi note numbers that complement the data. This piece of information is very useful particularly when engineering or tracking with musicians. In fact the midi note frequency chart is very helpful in understanding what range of notes are collated with which frequencies, and this can only be helpful to you when it comes to processing a mix. The chart clearly shows the relationships between pitch and frequency.

You do not need to learn this chart in parrot fashion but it is important to understand some of the frequencies that are used. Later when you use EQ to shape a sound or perhaps remove (or add) certain frequencies, the chart can prove to be very helpful..

In most cases, you only need to recognise the main frequencies for certain notes. For example: C4 at 261.63 Hz is a great reference point, because then you can find C5 or C3 very easily.

I cannot stress how important frequencies are for the understanding of sound and EQ. Engineers live by them as do producers and mastering engineers. If there is one piece of information that overrides any other in terms of importance it is the understanding of frequencies.

How often have you tried to mix your track only to be mystified by the result? Terms like 'muddy' or 'thin' spring to mind and these are all because the engineer or producer does not have an understanding of frequencies and their effect on other frequencies in a mix. Understand this basic concept and you will be armed with the most potent weapon.

Waveforms and frequencies go hand in hand. Understand these two and the rest is all about using the tools. So, let's get on with the chart.

Info

The more cycles per second, the higher the pitch. It is that simple.

Midi and frequency chart

You can see from the chart that for every octave you go up, you double the frequency - and it is the same in reverse; for every octave that you go down, you halve the frequency. The relationships between pitch and frequency are clearly evident in the chart.

Example: C4 is 261.63 Hz. To get to C5 we double the frequency so it is now 523.25Hz. And if we wanted to go from C4 to C3, it would be 130.81 Hz.

Now let us create the tag for this whole sound thing. I always imagine a

N	Midi Note	Frequency	N	Midi Note	Frequency
A0	21	27.500	F4	65	349.228
A#0	22	29.135	F#4	66	369.994
B0	23	30.868	G4	67	391.995
C1	24	32.703	G#4	68	415.305
C#1	25	34.648	A4	69	440.000
D1	26	36.708	A#4	70	466.164
Eb1	27	38.891	B4	71	493.883
E1	28	41.203	C5	72	523.251
F1	29	43.654	C#5	73	554.365
F#1	30	46.249	D5	74	587.330
G1	31	48.999	D#5	75	622.253
G#1	32	51.913	E5	76	659.255
A1	33	55.000	F5	77	698.456
A#1	34	58.270	F#5	78	739.989
B1	35	61.735	G5	79	783.991
C2	36	65.406	G#5	80	830.609
C#2	37	69.296	A5	81	880.000
D2	38	73.416	A#5	82	932.328
D#2	39	77.782	B5	83	987.767
E2	40	82.406	C6	84	1046.502
F2	41	87.307	C#6	85	1108.730
F#2	42	92.499	D6	86	1174.659
G2	43	97.999	D#6	87	1244.507
G#2	44	103.826	E6	88	1318.510
A2	45	110.000	F6	89	1396.913
A#2	46	116.541	F#6	90	1479.978
B2	47	123.471	G6	91	1567.982
C3	48	130.813	G#6	92	1661.219
C#3	49	138.591	A6	93	1760.000
D3	50	146.832	A#6	94	1864.655
D#3	51	155.563	B6	95	1975.533
E3	52	164.812	C7	96	2093.004
F3	53	174.614	C#7	97	2217.461
F#3	54	184.998	D7	98	2349.318
G3	55	195.997	D#7	99	2489.016
G#3	56	207.652	E7	100	2637.020
A3	57	220.000	F7	101	2793.826
A#3	58	233.082	F#7	102	2959.955
B3	59	246.942	G7	103	3135.963
C4	60	261.623	G#7	104	3322.437
C#4	61	277.183	A7	105	3520.000
D4	62	293.664	A#7	106	3729.310
D#4	63	311.127	B7	107	3951.066
E4	64	329.628	C8	108	4186.009

wave as a three dimensional entity, and with that I attach colours, speed and size. So, for a low frequency wave I will think of it as a large and flowing wave with nice warm colours like orange or deep red, and the whole image is nice and slow. For higher frequencies I use smaller and faster waves with harder colours like bright yellow or striking blue. This image is then enhanced further by having a person standing in front of the waves, usually me, but my name is Hertz and I am listening to these waves in a rental car. Although this may now confirm the urgency for me to seek therapeutic help, it is the best way for me to remember things.

You can create whatever images or story lines to the definitions in this tutorial. They are your images and must work for you.

Amplitude

Amplitude is the measurement of the displaced air (pressure), and in terms of audio this is perceived as loudness. Amplitude is actually the energy of sound or intensity/power.

I prefer the word waveform for sound as it is the form or shape that the waves take and the further we go into this tutorial the more that term will make sense as waveforms vary in shape and character. So, from now on, I will use the word waveform for sound where appropriate. It is better defined with a simple diagram. Figure 2.4 (consisting of a sine wave) is two cycles in length, and I have arrowed in the second cycle. It makes no difference which cycle I arrow as they are both repeats and identical in both shape and duration. The arrowed section deals with a single cycle.

The height or peak of the waveform is the amplitude and the length of the waveform is measured as two cycles. You can see the waveform starts at zero, goes up, drops to zero then goes to the negative area and then climbs to zero again. This is using the wave theory we defined earlier and all waveforms are represented like this.

I have arrowed a single cycle that does exactly what is described above: starts at 0, climbs to a positive value (peak of the amplitude), drops down to 0, then climbs down to a negative value and then back up to 0. If the waveform had no amplitude then it would be silent.

Figure 2.4
A two cycle sine wave

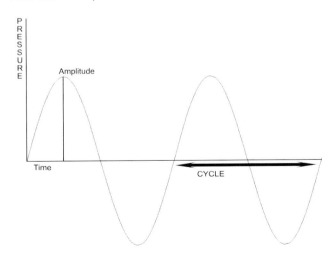

For now you do not need to worry about complex waveforms and any other factors regarding waveforms, as we will deal with them as we go along at your pace - that way you do not feel as if there is too much information to learn.

It is a fact that all waveforms are made up of sine waves at varying frequencies. This is not a crucial piece of information as far as EQ processing goes and is more useful for sound designers. But so long as you have a rudimentary understanding of what waveforms are and where they are derived from, you will be in a stronger position to visualise what needs doing to them. Understanding that waveforms are formed from sine waves will help you in all technical areas of this industry.

Understanding waveforms is another way of understanding the processes that need to be applied to them and how they are applied. Even though EQ can be applied to a single band or multi bands, it is very useful to know how the waveform behaves and what constitutes its makeup. This will then aid you in understanding how to best process the waveform.

Complex waveforms, by their very nature, need a slightly different approach when processing than single repeating raw waveforms like a sine wave (above in Figure 2.4).

Here is a little test for you to carry out. Look at Figure 2.4 and consider the following: If we had to calculate the average amplitude of the sine wave it would equal zero (0) since it rises and falls symmetrically above and below the axis. In fact if you were to take the sine wave, with its peaks and troughs (dips/valleys), and copy it onto itself you would simply get a louder sine wave. Now, if you were to shift one of the sine wave copies until its peak sat exactly over the dip of the original sine wave you would get silence. This is called 'total phase cancellation'. A single full cycle delay is referred to as a 360 degree phase. In this little test the phase is 180 degrees.

I know this sounds a little advanced but it is a good example of how a sine waveform behaves. Additionally, we will be touching on the subject of phase and offsets but not in terms of cancellation.

Hopefully the little test above will show you the relationship between the peaks and troughs of a sine waveform and how a simple phase shift can create silence. The idea of mixing two sine waves together that can be heard and ending up with silence does confuse people but it is an important piece of information to possess; phase cancellation comes up so often in audio engineering and having a rudimentary understanding of the concept will help greatly when using dynamic processing.

Definition time

The distance between one peak of a waveform to the next peak is called the wavelength.

The level or intensity of an audio signal (i.e. the loudness) is measured in decibels (dB) using the dB scale. 'Deci' being a tenth and 'Bel' being the unit.

A deep and moving question at this point is: 'Why do we measure in tenths and not in single units?' And the equally moving answer is: 'Our ears can hear a vast number of audio levels and it would be a mathematical nightmare to try to use the 'actual' numerical representations of audio levels - so we use tenths to make it easy to understand and calculate.

The true definition of dB is far more complicated and relative to ratio, logarithm of the ratio between two power levels etc, but all I want you to understand is that we measure audio level in dB.

The simplest way of explaining dB in terms of both hearing and measuring is to use the following:

Total silence is expressed as 0dB on the decibel scale. So if you had a sound that was ten times more powerful then it would be expressed as 10dB. That should be easy to understand. Where it gets a little confusing is that if you had a sound that was 100 times more powerful than total silence, it would be measured as 20dB. A sound 1000 times more powerful would be 30dB – and so on. We basically work on a logarithmic scale when dealing with dB.

However, I will keep it very simple and stick with dB simply being a way to measure loudness/level. If I state that at 30Hz I boosted by 3dB, then simply move the gain knob up by 3dB at that frequency. That is how simple I want to keep it.

SPL (sound pressure level)

While we are on the subject of hearing and decibels it is worth understanding SPL (sound pressure level). SPL is basically the acoustic pressure of a sound wave, measured in decibels above the threshold of hearing.

The human ear can accommodate a dynamic range of about 140dB, maximum. We define the threshold of hearing as 0dB SPL, and the point our ears explode (threshold of pain) as approximately 120-130 dB SPL.

The final most important component of sound is timbre.

Timbre

This is what defines the tonal quality of a sound. A C4 note played on a piano and at the same level as a C4 note played on a saxophone does not produce the same sound or timbre. They are both the same level and both played at C4, but both have distinctly different sounds or timbres.

Timbres are made up of waveforms and it is these waveforms that go to make up the tonal quality of a sound.

This is the main reason why one sound at a certain frequency can sound completely different to another sound at the exact same frequency.

When you come to use EQ you will understand why we do not have one overall frequency chart for all sounds. A female voice at C3 will sound completely different to a male voice at C3, so the EQ properties will have to be different as the timbres of the two sounds are distinctly different.

The first challenge when EQing musical sounds is in deciding which area of the frequency spectrum corresponds to which element of a sound's timbre. If you want to emphasize the attack of a bass drum, where should you boost? Alternatively, if your vocals sound boxy, where can you cut or boost most effectively?

Selecting a frequency range to process is crucial - this range (or the width of the range) is referred to as the bandwidth and is measured in Hertz.

As mentioned earlier we humans have a hearing range of between 20 Hz to 20 kHz and it is important to bear this in mind when processing certain sounds.

To be honest, anything at the 20 Hz level is felt more than heard, and this also applies to the higher range of frequencies (although excellent and true monitoring can reveal the 'air' range of frequencies).

Knowing that certain frequencies are felt as opposed to heard can be a really valuable piece of information. Some producers cleverly add lower frequencies to a track for that big club feel. Others will run a hi-pass filter at around the 20-40 Hz range to do the exact opposite as low level frequencies can be nauseating when 'felt' in a club environment.

The same thinking takes place for the very high frequency ranges. Boosting certain hi-range harmonic frequencies can help to add to the perception of space, sparkle and clarity. Of course, knowing which frequency ranges can be processed and which should be left alone is the real trick and I hope this book will help to alleviate some of the confusion associated with frequency management.

How to listen

At this point I would like to mention a very important aspect of conducting EQ tasks. To fully hear and feel the subtle changes in EQ you need two things: a great set of detailed headphones and an acoustically treated room.

The headphones will allow you to hear sound in isolation with the environment exhibiting no influence whatsoever on the sound. This is excellent for hearing very small detail on the quietest of sounds, and I regularly use headphones in tandem with monitors to detect and treat the smallest/quietest anomalies.

The room provides the overall listening of the sound and must be properly treated so as not to exhibit any bias or coloration of the sound, otherwise you are working blind/deaf. If you cannot truthfully and accurately hear what goes in, how can you treat what comes out?

The following is a piece I wrote about how sound travels in a room. Please pay close attention to the facts presented in the text as they are more relevant to you than to a professional producer working in a commercial studio with high-end acoustic treatment. The following tutorial is based on not having your studio acoustically treated, and is only a guide to try to maximize the best assets in mixing in a home studio.

Sound waves

Let us have a very brief look at how sound travels, and how we measure its effectiveness. Sound travels at approximately 1130 feet per second.

Now let us take a frequency travel scenario and try to explain its movement in a room. Let's look at a bass frequency of 60 Hz. When emitting sound, the speakers will vibrate 60 times per second. Each cycle (Hz) means that the speaker cones will extend forward when transmitting the sound, and retract back (rarefaction) when recoiling for the next cycle. These vibrations create peaks on the forward drive and troughs on the refraction. Each peak and trough equates to one cycle.

Imagine 60 of these every second. We can now calculate the wave cycles of this 60 Hz wave. We know that sound travels at approximately 1130 feet per second, so we can calculate how many wave cycles that is for the 60 Hz wave. We divide 1130 by 60, and the result is around 19 feet (18.83 if you want to be pedantic about it). We can now deduce that each wave cycle is 19 feet apart. To calculate each half cycle, i.e. the distance between the peak and trough, drive and rarefaction, we simply divide by two. We now have a figure of 9.5 feet. What that tells us is that if you sat anywhere up to 9.5 feet from your speakers, the sound would fly past you completely flat.

Reflected sound

However, this is assuming you have no boundaries of any sort in the room, i.e. no walls or ceiling. As we know that to be utter rubbish, we then need to factor in the boundaries.

These boundaries will reflect back the sound from the speakers and get mixed with the original source sound. This is not all that happens. The reflected sounds can come from different angles and because of their 'bouncing' nature could come at a different time from other waves. And because the reflected sound gets mixed with the source sound, the actual volume of the mixed wave is louder.

In certain parts of the room, the reflected sound will amplify because a peak might meet another peak (constructive interference), and in other parts of the room where a peak meets a trough (rarefaction), frequencies are cancelled out (destructive interference). Calculating what happens where is a nightmare.

In this scenario trying to make small EQ changes can be both deceptive and fruitless. This is why it is crucial for our ears to hear the sound from the speakers before they hear the reflective sounds. For argument's sake, I will call this sound 'primary' or 'leading', and the reflective sound 'secondary' or 'following'.

Our brains have the uncanny ability, due to an effect called the Haas effect, of both prioritizing and localising the primary sound, but only if the secondary sounds are low in amplitude. So, by eliminating as many of the secondary (reflective) sounds as possible, we leave the brain with the primary sound to deal with. This will allow for a more accurate location of the sound, and a better representation of the frequency content.

But is this what we really want? I ask this, because the secondary sound is also important in a 'real' space and goes to form the tonality of the sound being heard. Words like rich, tight and full all come from secondary sounds (reflected). So, we don't want to completely remove them as this would then give us a clinically dead space. We want to keep certain secondary sounds and only diminish the ones that really interfere with the sound.

Our brains also have the ability to filter or ignore unwanted frequencies. In the event that the brain is bombarded with too many reflections, it will have a problem localising the sounds, so it decides to ignore or suppress them.

The best example of this is when there is a lot of noise about you, like in a room or a bar, and you are trying to have a conversation with someone. The brain can ignore the rest of the noise and focus on 'hearing' the conversation you are trying to have. I am sure you have experienced this in public places, parties, clubs, football matches etc.

To carry that over to our real world situation of a home studio, we need to understand that reflective surfaces will create major problems, and the most common of these reflective culprits are walls. However, there is a way of overcoming this, assuming the room is not excessively reflective, and is the standard bedroom/living room type of space with carpet and curtains.

We overcome this with clever speaker placement and listening position, and before you go thinking that this is just an idea and not based on any scientific foundation, think again. The idea is to have the primary sound arrive at our ears before the secondary sound. Walls are the worst culprits, but because we know that sound travels at a given speed, we can make sure that the primary sound will reach our ears before the secondary sound does. By doing this, and with the Haas effect, our brains will prioritize the primary sound and suppress (if at low amplitude) the secondary sound, which will have the desired result, albeit not perfectly.

A room affects the sound of a speaker by the reflections it causes. We have covered this and now we need to delve a little more into what causes these reflections. Some frequencies will be reinforced, others suppressed, thus altering the character of the sound. We know that solid surfaces will reflect and porous surfaces will absorb, but this is all highly reliant on the materials being used.

Curtains and carpets will absorb certain frequencies, but not all, so it can sometimes be more damaging than productive. For this, we need to understand the surfaces that exist in the room. In our home studio scenario, we are assuming that a carpet and curtains, plus the odd sofa etc, are all that are in the room. We are not dealing with a steel factory floor studio.

In any listening environment, what we hear is a result of a mixture of both the primary and secondary (reflected) sounds. We know this to be true and our sound field will be a combination of both. In general, the primary sound from the speakers is responsible for the image, while the secondary sounds contribute to the tonality of the received sound.

The trick is to place the speakers in a location that will take of advantage of the desirable reflections while diminishing the unwanted reflection.

Headphones

Now let us touch on using headphones when mixing or processing. Good quality headphones can reveal details that some good speakers/monitors omit. In terms of sound processing, good headphones are imperative as they will be unforgiving in revealing anomalies. In terms of maintaining a clean and noise free signal path, they are crucial.

On the flip side, stereo imaging and panning information are much harder to judge on headphones. Determining the spatial feel of a mix is very difficult to convey on headphones, but far simpler with speakers. Pans are pronounced and extreme on headphones and do not translate across well. Even EQ can come across as subdued or extreme.

I find that if I mix on headphones alone, then the mix never travels well when auditioned with monitors. When using monitors and because the monitors are placed in front of us, our natural hearing perceives the soundstage as directly in front of us. With headphones, because the 'speakers' are on either side of us, there's no real front-to-back information.

Headphones also provide a very high degree of separation between the left and right channels, which produces an artificially detailed stereo image.

Our brains and ears receive and analyze/process sound completely differently when using headphones as opposed to monitors. When using head-

Info

The idea is to have the primary sound arrive at our ears before the secondary sound.

Info

The trick is to place the speakers in a location that will take of advantage of the desirable reflections while diminishing the unwanted reflections.

Tip

Pans are pronounced and extreme on headphones and do not translate across well.

phones, each ear will only hear the audio carried on the relevant channel, but when listening to a pair of speakers in a room, both ears will hear the signals produced by both the left and right loudspeakers. The timing differences associated with this acoustic 'crosstalk' between the two channels and each ear lie at the core of the 'stereo illusion'.

You also need to factor in the fact that different people perceive different amounts of bass – factors such as the distance between the headphone diaphragm and the listener's ear will change the level of bass. The way in which the headphone cushion seals around the ear also plays a part, which is why pushing the headphones closer to your ears produces a noticeable increase in bass. This increases the bass energy and this alone negates the idea of having correct tonal balance in the mix being auditioned. Trying to EQ with bias to any frequency demotes the whole process as useless.

With monitors both ears hear both the left and right channels. When listening to ordinary stereo material via headphones, we have only the differences in level between the two channels to go on, and hence the stereo images become non-linear and ill-defined. In fact, most people perceive the individual sound sources to lie on a line running directly through the centre of the head, instead of being portrayed in front of us as they would be with loudspeakers. This radically different presentation is what makes judging stereo signals and panning mono ones so much more difficult on headphones.

If your room is acoustically problematic and you have poor monitors, then headphones may well be a better and more reliable approach. But it is a lot harder to achieve the same kind of quality and transferability that comes more naturally on good monitors in a good acoustically treated room.

I find that if I record and check all my signals with headphones, then I am in a strong position to hear any anomalies and be in a better position to judge clarity and integrity of the recorded signals. This, coupled with speaker monitoring, assures me of the best of both worlds; clarity and integrity married with spatial imaging.

Ultimately, any processing that you conduct will require a truthful (accurate) listening environment, be it headphones or acoustically treated room or, preferably, both. When dealing with EQ this becomes even more vital as EQ usually entails processing with very small changes and these changes can be almost inaudible in the bigger picture of a mix. In an acoustically treated room with good frequency and flat monitors, EQ changes of less than 1 dB can be heard.

The whole of this chapter has been written to offer you an insight into how crucial the 'listening' experience/environment is particularly when dynamic processing with small changes comes into play.

EQ adjustments are not about huge sweeping changes to a sound but about subtle changes that can either define a sound or colour it. A poor room and poor headphones will offer an inaccurate presentation of the sound that needs processing.

A little understanding of the dynamics and physics of how sound travels in a given environment can only be an asset to you. I hope this chapter goes a little way in helping you to bend your head around how sound travels in an environment and how you can get the most out of the listening process.

Fundamentals and harmonics

One thing that can help a little in deciding which frequencies need processing is to know what frequencies correspond to the fundamentals of each musical pitch. For a start, this allows you to define the lower limit of the range of frequencies generated by pitched sounds.

When using EQ it is important to understand the concepts of fundamentals and harmonics. So, let's talk a little about harmonics. First, the emotional definition or description:

- All musical tones have a complex waveform, made up of lots of different frequencies. All sounds are formed using a combination of sine waves at varying frequencies and amplitudes (discussed earlier).

If we look at the frequencies of a complex waveform, then the lowest frequency is called the fundamental frequency. The fundamental frequency determines the pitch of the sound. The higher frequencies are called overtones. If the overtones are multiples of the fundamental frequency (x1, x2, x3 etc) then they are called harmonics. The overtones or upper partials (as some people like to refer to them) must be multiples of the fundamental to be known as harmonics. These frequencies and their amplitudes determine the timbre of a sound.

Now, the simpler explanation:

- If you have a waveform that has a fundamental frequency of 100 kHz, then the second harmonic will be 200 kHz and the third harmonic will be 300 kHz and so on...

Since we know that complex waveforms are created with sine waves at different frequencies and amplitudes, it then follows that a sine wave that adds the second harmonic and third harmonic to itself will then form a complex waveform. Try it.

Noise

However, the exception to this rule is an irregular waveform like noise. If you think about the irregular waveform of noise then you will understand that it has no harmonics. Noise contains a wide band of frequencies and it is generally accepted that, at waveform level, there are no harmonics as the waveform is non-repeating.

I have found that by boosting certain sounds below their fundamental frequency, noise of some sort is introduced into the mix. This piece of information usually lies by the wayside and is rarely touched on. Understanding the lower limit is always extremely handy when it comes to EQ as boosting below the fundamental can create anomalies like noise. By understanding the harmonic content of a sound, or how the harmonics are created, it can help when it comes to EQing a sound in a mix.

But it doesn't end there as EQing certain harmonics can change the perception of what is heard at another fundamental. It is also important to understand the relationship between the fundamental and the harmonic as it can get confusing as to which one needs to be processed to attain the optimum result. When dealing with very low frequencies, the fundamental/harmonic choice can get a little confusing. In cases where it is hard to distinguish between the fundamental and harmonic it pays to use the most potent weapons at your disposal … your ears!

EQ is not always about detailed analysis and sometimes requires a more 'general' approach of listening to the overall 'effect' of the sound. It is about 'what sounds right'.

The concept of harmonics, fundamentals, overtones etc seems daunting; but it's not! The above is simply to give you a better and more thorough insight into what sound and all of its components are.

In terms of EQ processing, it is vital to understand that the basic concepts of sound, fundamentals and harmonics are particularly important, as EQing a sound's fundamental/harmonic can have a significant effect on the perception of another sound's fundamental/harmonic; and of course, its own.

Every sound is defined by its fundamental and the amplitude of the harmonics. These qualities determine if a sound is that of a piano or violin.

Below is a list with approximate figures for instrument frequency ranges and their fundamentals and harmonics. As I said earlier, due to their inaccuracy I do not like lists that purport to be an accurate frequency range table for varying instruments. However, this list is simply to help you understand the fundamental and harmonic frequencies of a selection of instruments.

I have tried to keep the list varied but not specific to 'type' (orchestral, dance etc). These figures are only guides, and to be used purely as such.

Instrument	Fundamentals	Harmonic
Kick Drum	30–145 Hz	1–6 kHz
Snare Drum	100–200 Hz	1–20 kHz
Cymbal	300–580 Hz	1–15 kHz
Acoustic Bass	40–295 Hz	1–5 kHz
Electric Bass	40–300 Hz	1–7 kHz
Acoustic Guitar	82–988 Hz	1–15 kHz
Electric Guitar	82–1319 Hz	1–15 kHz
Piano	28–4196 Hz	5–8 kHz
Bass Voice	87–392 Hz	1–12 kHz
Alto Voice	175–698 Hz	2–12 kHz
Soprano Voice	247–1175 Hz	2–12 kHz

To cut or to boost?

This is a debate that will go on forever. There are arguments for both sides and it will eventually come down to personal choice. However, there are certain reasons for adopting either and I hope this chapter will help in clarifying and simplifying this confusing subject.

A common problem that beginners make is to boost frequencies in a mix to try to make it stand out more. This is true particularly for drum sounds. The problem here is that noise inherent in the audio signal is also boosted, so what you end up with is a noisy sound in the mix, which stands out even more than intended. Additionally, because one sound has been boosted the others seem tame in volume compared to the boosted signal. So the beginner tries to compensate by boosting other sounds to attain an even balance. Yep, you guessed it, more noise.

Headroom

But let us assume that noise is not an issue and that the audio being boosted is clean. The problem that is inherent now is the lack of headroom. When you boost any signal in a digital domain you eat up the headroom and generally raise the noise floor. Boost beyond the headroom and the signal will clip and, trust me, you do not want digital clipping. This is not the same as driving a signal in an analogue domain (mixer) whereby the ceiling can be exceeded and pleasant harmonic distortion achieved (depending on the mixer). Digital is unforgiving and lives by certain finite laws that cannot be bent.

If you have allowed for ample headroom in your audio channels, then boosting by small amounts is not a problem – but so many beginners believe the 'louder the better' thinking that they can peak the audio signal as close to the ceiling as possible, but any boosts that take place either clip the channel or, when summed to a stereo mix, clip the main stereo outputs.

Think of headroom as follows: You are 6 foot tall and the room you are entering has a 7 foot ceiling height. You have 1 foot of headroom. In terms of an audio signal, headroom is the difference between the maximum signal level and the maximum limit of its environment/device. In the digital domain we know that the ceiling is 0 dBFS, and anything beyond this incurs digital clipping (nasty).

Info

A common problem that beginners make is to boost frequencies in a mix to try to make it stand out more. The problem here is that noise inherent in the audio signal is also boosted.

Overall level

'Overall level' is another problem that arises from multiple EQ boosts. The fact that EQ is boosted at a certain frequency means that the overall gain of the mix that the sound resides in is also boosted. So, whenever you perform EQ tasks, compensate the overall level of the mix. Make sure to compensate at every stage and not to leave it at the end. Small changes always add up to a big result, so keep this in mind when using EQ on individual sounds within in a mix.

There is another reason why it is best to use cut than boost. We will eventually come to see how EQ works and the different types of EQ, but since we are on the subject of cut versus boost it is relevant to consider the following: When using certain types of resonant filters on narrow frequency ranges (peak EQ) it is generally better to cut, as boosting will impart a 'ringing' type of effect on the frequency range.

If the bandwidth is very narrow then it can pay to cut, but this is reliant on the type of EQ being used. It can be beneficial to use a wider frequency range (band) and then to boost by small amounts. This works particularly well when using EQ in a mix context. I will sometimes EQ the 'air' frequencies of a mix by using a very small boost on that particular range. This is far less obtrusive than larger boosts at narrower frequencies.

The true art of EQ is to cut, not boost. However, boosting certain frequencies by small amounts can have a distinct impact on a mix that might be required. The trick is to know when to cut and when to boost.

To be able to instinctively know when to cut (roll-off) or boost, you need to understand frequencies. The relationships between frequencies of sounds within a mix are a great example of how frequencies can clash or mask.

- A bass might sound great on its own but when you add a low frequency pad to it in the mix, it can start to sound muddy. Cutting certain shared frequencies from one of the sounds can open up the range and allow the other sound to 'breathe'.
- A piano and mid frequency string can drown each other in a mix and offer no depth or width. Boosting the low-end of the piano sound might add that vital lower end frequency range missing from the combined sounds and actually enrich the combination.

This is the Art; knowing when to cut and when to boost, and this is achieved through knowledge and experience. It is also Bible that when one sound is treated, another sound will be affected in a mix, not physically but in terms of perception.

Cutting higher frequencies obviously makes the sound 'bassier' - this is the nature of sound. Remove lower frequencies and the sound will sound brighter. This is how hi-fi systems used to work in the old days of simple graphic equalisers. Cut one frequency and the whole tonal content of a sound or mix changes. With this in mind it does not follow that boosting is right or cutting is right. This process depends on a number of factors, the primary one being that of headroom and noise floor.

Info

The true art of EQ is to cut, not boost.

By understanding the nature and characteristics of the sound, be it in a mix context or in isolation, you can then understand the processes required to dynamically change the sound. More importantly, understanding a mix in the context of all the sound elements is really what all producers and engineers strive towards.

The simple process of understanding where a sound lies in the entire frequency spectrum of a mix is as important as understanding the process to alter it.

Example

If you strip down this thinking to an example that entails only processing two sounds then you will understand how crucial this is. A good example would be to take two sounds that share frequencies such as a violin and a cello. A cello will normally have a frequency range of 65 Hz – 2 kHz. A violin will normally have a frequency range of 195 Hz – 3.5 kHz.

As you can clearly see they both share common frequencies between 195 Hz – 2 kHz.

If you were to cut between 2 and 3 kHz by 3dB on the violin, then the two together would sound deeper as the top-end has been attenuated (reduced). In this instance the cello would sound more dominant.

If you were to cut between 65 and 200 Hz on the cello then the two together would sound brighter. In this instance the violin would be more pronounced.

I call this 'complementary or compensatory processing'.

Mid range frequencies

The one area that is always the hardest to learn is the mid-range frequencies. With so many sounds sharing this part of the frequency spectrum, it can be confusing to find a good balance of frequencies in a mix.

The mid-range frequency spectrum is the most important for any song, as the vocals, guitars, pianos etc will invariably share common frequencies and predominantly lie in this frequency range. When I have to mix a song, and EQ is going to be used, I always start with the mid frequency range and work from there. Once you have this area sorted out then referencing the high and low ranges becomes a lot easier. In effect, you manage the dominant range of frequencies and then reference the high and low ranges to that. If you start with either of the extremes and then try to process the mid-range you will invariably end up having to compensate.

There is another reason that working outwards from the mid-range is such a good idea, and it has to do with both perception and how the ears and brain attune themselves to a range of frequencies as a reference. Let me put it in another way: if you start to work on the high frequencies, within a certain period your ears and brain will stabilise the hearing range to accommodate the higher frequencies. In other words the high-end becomes the standard for the ear/brain. They have attuned themselves to this range as 'normal'. This will invariably have the effect of making the other frequency ranges very pronounced. The mid and low ranges now become very pronounced and you will end up trying to compensate for those frequencies. You will then

Info

The mid-range frequency spectrum is the most important for any song, as the vocals, guitars and pianos fall in this frequency range.

attain the result of a very trebly mix. This thinking is also applied to mixing in general.

I always advise my students to listen to a well produced and mastered commercial track prior to any mixing projects as the ears/brain will attune themselves to the frequencies and how well they are processed. This then acts as a reference for their mix project. In terms of hearing, they will have a good foundation to work from.

The same applies to EQ processing. If you work from the mid-range your ears/brain will not have to try to accommodate any extremes of frequencies, and referencing to this range is far more natural and comfortable for the ears and brain.

Applying EQ to a stereo mix

Applying overall general EQ to a stereo mix is not always the answer to shaping the mix. Sometimes you need to go back to the individual mix elements (sounds) and tweak each sound, as detailed processing of distinct frequency ranges (bands) can be far more beneficial for the overall mix than an EQ process on the mix itself.

In this instance it is imperative to understand the relationships between the sounds in terms of both frequency range and amplitude. However, this is not always the case. Quite often applying gentle EQ to a final mix can have the desired 'genre' effect, or can be pleasing when using certain types of EQs that exhibit more 'colour' than precision - analogue EQs would be a good example.

Another mistake that is so common amongst beginners is the notion that boosting a frequency range that does not exist will be a solution to a problem. A good example of this is boosting high-end frequencies in a dull mix in the hope that it will 'brighten' the mix or add more 'sparkle. This is nonsense as all that is achieved is that noise and certain artefacts are introduced into the mix. The boost simply results in boosting these artefacts and noise and not the existing frequencies. The result is a hard and dirty/gritty mix. You cannot cut or boost frequencies that are not there.

Of course there are technical restrictions to how an EQ is to be used, and we have covered some of these and will cover more later. But generally speaking it is a tool, and how you use that tool is up to you.

Grouped sounds

The same applies to 'grouped' sounds. Grouped sounds could be complementary sounds that will often share frequencies, or are sounds that are grouped together like drum sounds that form a kit or the drum loop. When processing grouped sounds it is important to understand the nature of each sound within the group and how it will react to EQ. In like-for-like grouped sounds such as a drum kit, an overall EQ process might yield a certain result that was being aimed for; giving the whole drum beat a little more punch and clarity. Sometimes, it is the individual sounds in the drum kit that need processing, i.e. adding more snap to a snare whilst adding a little lower end to the kick.

Info

You cannot cut or boost frequencies that are not there.

I have often grouped all the low-end sounds to a single group channel and then rolled off a very low range to remove muddiness. So, it's not just about like-for-like sounds, but similar frequencies too. I have also grouped complementary sounds such as the whole mid-range to a group channel and then applied some gentle EQ to pronounce this entire range as a whole, as opposed to trying to process each sound individually. It really comes down to what you are trying to achieve and adopting the best means to attain the result that you want. But generally, unless the above is in force, I will always EQ sounds individually within a mix context.

This is why cutting or boosting small amounts around distinct frequency spectrums of individual sounds can be so much more effective than choosing an overall frequency range for a number of sounds and altering that.

Loudness

It doesn't end there. EQ can be used to alter the apparent loudness of a mix, a technique commonly used by mastering houses. EQ is not always about reshaping a sound/mix but about controlling the amplitudes of frequency bands. If this band encompasses the whole mix then an EQ can be used to alter the amplitude of the whole mix and add colour.

I have on occasion run my entire mix through a flat-lined EQ (usually an analogue hardware EQ) and adjusted the gain. This affords me the colour of the EQ being used and obviously boosting the gain. It is not a practice I often employ, for a number of reasons, primarily that there are better gain structuring tools than a flat-lined EQ. EQ will also exhibit certain anomalies if used incorrectly.

Remember, EQ is also about perception. The frequency response of our hearing system changes with loudness. It is important to monitor at a realistic and sensible volume when applying EQ, because the perceived effect may be quite different at higher or lower listening levels.

However, the higher the intensity of the sound, the more sensitive to high and low frequencies the ear gets; this means any sound comparatively rich in these frequencies is interpreted as 'loud' by the brain. Therefore, if you want music to sound louder at low listening levels, then it makes sense to boost at the extremes of the frequency range. This is what some hi-fi systems do when the 'Boost' or 'Loudness' button is used. In most playback systems, you will see what is referred to as the 'smile' curve on graphic EQs, and it is for the reasons outlined above. The smile shape denotes that there is a dip in the mid frequencies and small boosts in the extreme frequencies (low and high). Always be aware as to the difference between 'actual' and 'perceived'.

It is also true to state that at low listening levels, the human hearing system encounters difficulties hearing very low and very high frequencies. This is called the Fletcher Munson Effect. In this instance, EQ is used to cut and boost selected frequencies, so that a more balanced gain structure is kept throughout the hearing spectrum at low listening levels.

Distance effect

Apart from the obvious qualities that have already been covered, it is worth considering EQ's relationship to and with distance. A brighter sound, or a

Tip

If you want music to sound louder at low listening levels, then it makes sense to boost at the extremes of the frequency

sound that contains high frequency energy, will sound further away than a sound with lower frequencies. The reason for this is that air acts as a 'dampener' (filtering frequencies) and this dampening effect is most noticeable at higher frequencies. The further the sound has to travel the more it gets dampened. Low frequency sounds are affected far less.

Using this piece of information it follows that if you filter out (cut) high frequencies from a mix the mix sounds more upfront and closer. In fact, this technique has been successfully used to bring certain sounds in a mix closer (front) or further away (back). If you have pre-recorded vocals with a lot of room ambience then simply EQing a selected range of high frequencies can give the impression that the room ambience has been removed and the vocals will sound closer (corrective EQ).

Masking

Masking is another problem that can be treated with sensible use of EQ. How many times have you used a sound that on its own sounds excellent, but gets swallowed up when placed alongside another sound? This happens because the two sounds have very similar frequencies and one is at a higher level; hence one 'masks', or hides, the other sound. This results in the masked sound sounding dull, or just simply unheard. EQ is a very good tool to use in these instances. By cutting away certain frequencies from one of the sounds, you will invariably expose and boost the frequencies of the other sound, thus accomplishing separation and distinction between the two sounds.

Another pitfall that most beginners (and some pros) fall into is what I call the EQ syndrome. This happens when a mix is poorly recorded with little separation in the sounds and EQ is used to try to 'separate' and 'cleanse' the sounds. This always results in a brittle mix with individual sound components sounding as if they do not belong together. Another example of this EQ syndrome is when an engineer or producer feels that they have to EQ every channel to gain a stamp on their 'feel'. This complaint is quite common in certain Hip Hop and Dance songs whereby the drive (drum beat and bass line) of the song sounds separate from the vocals. This can actually be a good thing, if the effect is intended, but the ear begins to attune itself to the separate frequency bands instead of a combination of a rich tapestry of frequencies, and the song then starts to 'tire' the listener.

Long EQ sessions

Finally, when conducting long EQ sessions the ear and brain continually try to attune themselves to new references and eventually tire, and this can result in overuse of EQ to compensate for areas of the spectrum that are thought to need processing. Try to work in short sessions when mixing and processing and give the ears a chance to rest and the brain to 'unscramble'.

In these instances it is crucial to have a clean and balanced recording so that the EQ process can be creative as opposed to corrective. You should strive to record the source sound elements at near enough the frequencies that you will eventually release. That way you will only need to make minor adjustments instead of sweeping corrections.

The added advantage of a clean and balanced recording, with emphasis

Tip

Try to work in short sessions when mixing and processing and give the ears a chance to rest and the brain to 'unscramble'.

on the correct source frequencies, is that you can always come back and remix the entire recording off a blank palette. The recording will never tire itself and never be constricted in terms of frequencies. This will always allow for refreshing remixes.

If a frequency range is too narrow and boosted it can be painful for the listener, in the same way as over compression can tire a mix and make it sterile. The same can be said of all the frequencies as in a mix context. Narrow banding a mix is as destructive as square wave compression. Both will tire the listener.

Dynamic range is the difference between the quietest parts of a sound (troughs) in relation to the loudest (peaks). In other words: the difference in volume level between the quietest and loudest parts of a signal. Over-compression, by its very nature, compromises the dynamic range of a signal and narrow bands the whole signal (bringing the peaks and troughs closer together). This has the effect of being constant, uninteresting and tiring the listener. The brain is most active in hearing when it has dynamic range to deal with. Subtle gain changes across a wide spread of frequencies keep the brain active in constantly evaluating and re-evaluating the information it receives.

The same can be said for EQ. Narrow banding frequencies made by boosting and cutting wrong frequencies can result in the same outcome as over-compression. A brittle or muddy mix means that there is overemphasis on the higher or lower end frequencies. This in turn can be exhausting to the listener as the brain tries to adjust to these references and has no variety to readjust or retune itself to.

Keep your EQ tasks interesting and varied. Slamming the low-end on a club track does not mean it will be attractive. After the ears and brain have attuned themselves to these limited frequencies they will simply switch off; then the nerves take over.

The object of using EQ on a mix is to remove problematic frequencies, separate sounds, gel sounds and finally to provide a rich and varied tapestry of frequencies for the listener to constantly 'think' about. How you achieve this comes down to selection of EQ and whether to cut or to boost. Knowledge, experience and your ears will tell you which is best for a given task at any given time.

For your own sanity, and experience, I suggest you try both boost and cut on a test mix and try to evaluate the results. Slowly but surely your ears will attune themselves to what is 'right' and your brain will 'know' what and how to achieve the 'right'.

Digital EQ vs Analogue EQ

Finally, I would like to mention the primary difference between using a digital EQ plug-in and its analogue hardware counterpart. Some digital EQs exhibit sonic-side effects when boosting, particularly at the higher frequencies. Analogue EQs processing side effects are far more musical as they are designed to impart 'colour' very simply through the processing. This is why certain analogue hardware EQs will have a certain 'character' and impart their tonal 'colour' onto the sound being processed.

Many producers will carry in their studios a combination of digital EQ plug-ins used more for corrective processes and transparency, and analogue hardware EQs for their 'colour' and musical tonal shaping qualities. There are some excellent top-end digital EQ plug-ins that are both accurate in their coding and processing and transparent. But for sheer musicality I prefer to use analogue EQs.

The many guises of EQ

Corrective EQ

We use corrective EQ on a particular sound, frequency or recording to isolate and diminish a frequency or sound (i.e. remove problematic frequencies) or to accentuate or elevate (separation and emphasis).

Classic cases are that of broadcast engineers having to isolate the narrative or spoken part amidst a plethora of background noises, or to simply remove a click or unwanted sound, and, even more commonly, to alter the spoken part to sound more pleasing. The latter is more in the domain of creative or musical EQ, but in most cases the two forms will cross paths and share objectives.

EQ to separate tracks

Using EQ as a tool to separate tracks is another favourite of producers. This is actually quite an important procedure, but one that does need a careful approach. It is imperative that your recordings are as clean as possible and have a perfect signal-to-noise (S/N) ratio. This will ensure that small amounts of EQ boost on selective frequencies will attain the best results.

A lot of beginners make the mistake of poorly recording the source material and then using EQ to try to separate and boost the gains of the recorded tracks. Separation can only be truly affected if there is a clear distinction between frequencies, so that you need to isolate only small frequency ranges and apply nominal cuts or boosts. Having a muddy mix of low-end instruments means having to perform some extreme cuts/boosts, and this will be more destructive than creative.

Another area of separation that is very important is that of redundant frequencies. This is my very flash way of saying 'frequencies that are not needed'. You will find that there are a lot of instruments that share low frequencies, not just basses and kick drums. So removing predefined low frequency ranges from some of the low-end instruments in your mix can actually separate and define the low frequencies even more. This is, of course, corrective EQ.

Recording your tracks rich in frequencies allows you the scope to cut or boost any frequency range as it already exists in the recorded audio. Remember the rule: you cannot boost or cut frequencies that do not exist.

Separating the frequencies of instruments by the use of EQ is a traditional yet subtle method of creative and corrective EQ. In fact, this method is not limited to the mix and production stages but is also prevalent at the tracking stage. There are many instances whereby EQ has to be used to compensate for a poor microphone (or its use in a given environment), or a poor room (poor acoustics resulting in boomy, resonant or ringing anomalies).

EQ in live situations

EQ is also used in live situations to compensate for the environment, the singer, the microphone, background noise, colour and so on. Again, corrective and creative EQ cross paths, but invariably corrective is always the first goal followed by creative (this is dealt with later when discussing Primary and Secondary EQ).

Creative EQ

Creative EQ is an art form in itself. It is used to add an overall shape and colour to a sound/mix, to bring out certain aesthetic qualities that corrective EQ cannot, and to enhance the listening experience by creating a pre selected perception. Examples of this include:

• Bringing out the best in a lead vocal line and yet keeping it balanced with the backing vocals
• Mixing the drive element of a track to its optimum club feel
• Using coloured EQs to add to or alter an existing sound

Mixing for a genre entails certain types of processing and EQ plays a huge part in achieving the perception that the genre needs. Creative EQ plays a dominant role in achieving this perception. Using EQ to add harmonic transients to a sound is purely creative but does entail following the 'corrective rules'. The list is endless. You are only limited by your knowledge on the subject, and of course, having an ear helps but this is not a prerequisite.

EQ at the mastering stage

Finally we use EQ at the mastering stage to best represent the final stereo mix for its genre and medium. Once all the elements are in place and a mix of the session is handed to the mastering house, the real treatment takes place. Here we bring out the best in the final mix, make sure that there is a good dynamic range and ensure all the elements are in place for whatever market the mix is aimed (including the medium it is to be played through). EQ plays a crucial role in this process not just to enhance the master and best portray the frequency spread but to correct any existing anomalies.

A well mastered mix will not need any additional EQ manipulating at the listening stage, as good mastering houses will treat the signal for optimum use on all listening mediums. A good mastering house/engineer can make or break your track in the commercial vein. Their most valued weapon is EQ.

So, we now understand how important EQ is and the fundamental uses it might have, but we have not delved into the different types of EQ available. We will do this in chapter 9, but first let's get some important definitions out of the way.

Filters

To further understand the terminology used in this book, I feel it is essential that you understand the following terms:

Cut-off frequency
This is the point (frequency) at which the filter begins to 'filter' (block or cut out). The filter will lower the volume of the frequencies above or below the cut-off frequency depending on the type of filter used.

Attenuation
This 'lowering of the volume of the frequencies,' is called Attenuation. In the case of a low-pass filter, the frequencies above the cut-off are attenuated. In the case of a high-pass filter, the frequencies below the cut-off are attenuated.

Resonance
Boosting the narrow band of frequencies at the cut-off point is called resonance. Also know as Q and bandwidth, in effect, the higher the resonance, the narrower the bandwidth.

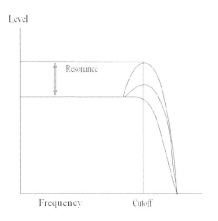

Figure 7.1
Resonance

Q
Also known as 'width of the filter response', this is the 'centre frequency' of the bandwidth and is measured in Hz. Also know as bandwidth and resonance. A high Q value denotes a narrow filter width (bandwidth). A low Q value denotes a wide filter width (bandwidth).

This is actually a very important piece of information because with the Q control alone you can make your audio sound high and brittle or warm and musical. This does not mean that you must use low Q values all the time, in the hope of attaining warmth, but you must understand what frequencies need filtering. If your intent is to use EQ as a musical tool, then be aware of what the Q value can do to audio. For creative EQ, this is a weapon often ignored.

Slope
'Slope' is the rate at which a high or low frequency EQ section reduces the level above or below the cut-off frequency. The shape and parameters are denoted as dB per octave and are usually: 6, 12, 18 or 24dB/octave. Slope also determines the characteristic of the filter and can range from smooth to extreme (gentle to aggressive).

HF
High (hi) frequency.

LF
Low (lo) frequency.

Mid
Mid frequency.

Cut
To reduce the level of a signal using a filter. To lower the frequency amplitude of a band.

Boost
To apply gain or to increase by level. Measured in dB.

Band
A single filter in an equaliser or a range of pre determined frequencies.

Centre frequency
The frequency at which a peaking filter applies maximum gain.

Filter
A circuit which alters the level of a limited range of frequencies.

Octave
Doubling of a frequency (explained earlier).

Filter shapes

Bell
An EQ with a peak in its response denoted by its shape and quite common nowadays on most virtual EQs. The bell shape has symmetrical response

characteristics. In other words it has the same response whether boosting or cutting.

Shelf

A high or low frequency EQ where the response extends from the selected frequency to the highest or lowest frequency values in the audio range.

Low-pass and high-pass

A low-pass shelving filter passes all frequencies below its cut-off frequency, but attenuates all frequencies above its cut-off frequency. Similarly, a high-pass filter passes all frequencies above its cut-off frequency, but affects all frequencies below its cut-off frequency.

Figure 7.2
Filter shapes

Types of EQ

To begin to understand the EQ, we need to first define the two categories it falls into; passive and active.

Passive EQs

These types of EQs have the distinction of being extremely simple in design and, more importantly, they cannot boost frequencies, only cut. The way they work is actually very much to do with perception. For example, by cutting low frequencies (bass) they make the mid and high frequencies sound 'louder'.

Passive EQs do have their uses. Although they are inflexible, they can perform reduction tasks reasonably well. By cutting high frequencies, they are able to cut or lower hiss (high frequency noise). However by their very nature, passive EQs or filters then need to have the signal boosted to compensate for the cut. This in itself introduces noise into the signal path; the noise coming from the amp used to boost the signal.

In terms of circuitry, passive equalisers place the equalization circuits either before or after a fixed-gain amplifier, in which case the amp makes up for the inherent loss in the EQ circuit, effectively boosting the frequency range(s) that haven't been cut.

Active EQs

Because of the limitations of passive EQs, most EQs are built around active filter circuits which use frequency selective components, together with a low noise amplifier. And it is this type of EQ that we are going to concentrate on.

Fixed frequency EQ

Pretty self explanatory, this EQ allows cut/boost of one or more frequencies. There are no additional controls over the usual components, like bandwidth, Q, etc.

Peaking EQ

A peaking EQ is an EQ which boosts a specific band of frequencies. Whereas a shelving filter has a shelf like curve, this filter has a bell shaped curve. The Q setting determines the width of the bell, while boost or cut determines the height or depth of the bell.

Figure 8.1
Peaking EQ (filter). The shape of the
frequency response resembles a peak.

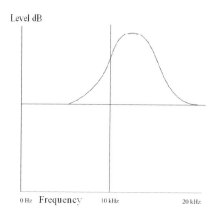

Figure 8.1
Peaking EQ (filter). The shape of the
frequency response resembles a peak.

Two band or three band

These types of EQ simply have two or three separate frequency ranges. Usually denoted as low, mid and high, these bands can only be cut or boosted.

Shelving filter/EQ

We have touched on the use of tone controls as forms of EQ. These controls control a type of filter that is called a shelving filter. In the case of the bass and treble knobs, low-pass and hi-pass shelving filters are used respectively.

A low-pass shelving filter passes all frequencies below its cut-off frequency, but attenuates all frequencies above its cut-off frequency. Similarly, a high-pass filter passes all frequencies above its cut-off frequency, but affects all frequencies below its cut-off frequency.

This is the simplest type of active EQ. This EQ can shape response in a number of ways: boost/cut low frequencies, boost/cut high frequencies. This is why I have included the diagram to demonstrate what happens with the filters, low and hi-pass, in this type of EQ. Most mixers will allow for low and high frequency EQ, and in the case of shelving filters, their mid frequencies are usually fixed.

It is also common for the filter slope to be 6 dB per octave. This allows for a gentler effect. The shape is 'shelf-like', so the boost or cut is progressive over a range. Filters do not have zero effect at a particular frequency and then instantly jump and suddenly reappear at the next frequency; they have to get there

Figure 8.2
Shelving EQ (filter). The shape of the
frequency response resembles a shelf.

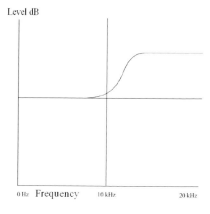

somehow. The way they do so, and by how much, is called the gradient or slope. In the case of the shelving filter, the most common slope is 6 dB gain change per octave (doubling of the frequency). It takes time for the filter to attenuate frequencies in proportion to the distance from the cut-off point; this is the slope.

Shelving filters are generally designed to apply equal gain changes beyond the shelving frequency and have controls for selecting the shelf, cut and boost. The figures below illustrate what happens if you cut or boost frequencies in a low-pass and a hi-pass filter.

As Figures 8.3 and 8.4 clearly show; in the low-pass filter diagram the frequencies below the cut-off are allowed to pass through whereas the frequencies above the cut-off are attenuated. In the high-pass filter the frequencies below the cut-off are attenuated and the frequencies above the cut-off are allowed to pass through.

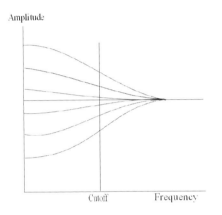

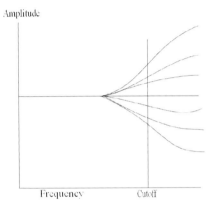

Figure 8.3
Low pass filter.

Figure 8.4
High pass filter.

Graphic EQ

A graphic equalizer is simply a set of filters, each with a fixed centre frequency that cannot be changed. The only control you have is the amount of boost or cut in each frequency band. This boost or cut is most often controlled with sliders. The sliders are a graphic representation of the frequency response, hence the name 'graphic' equalizer.

The more frequency bands you have, the more control and accuracy you have over the frequency response. Mixing consoles rarely have graphic EQs, but PA mixers often have a stereo graphic EQ for EQing the final stereo output.

Band-pass filter

A graphic equalizer uses a set of band-pass filters that are designed to completely isolate certain frequency bands. The diagram below shows the frequency response of a band-pass filter.

This is a great filter. It attenuates frequencies below and above the cut-off and leaves the frequencies at the cut-off. It is in effect a low-pass and a hi-pass together. The cool thing about this filter is that you can eliminate the lower and

Figure 8.5
Band-pass filter. A filter that passes frequencies between two limits is known as a band-pass filter.

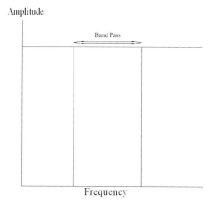

higher frequencies and be left with a band of frequencies that you can then use as either an effect (as in having that real mid-range type of old radio sound), or use it for isolating a narrow band of frequencies in recordings that have too much low and high-end.

Try this filter on synthesizer sounds and you will come up with some wacky sounds. It really is a useful filter and if you can run more than one at a time, and select different cut-offs for each one; then you will get even more interesting results. Band-pass filtering is used on formant filters that you find on so many softsynths, plug-ins, synthesizers and samplers – Emu/Ensoniq are known for some of their format filters and that technology is based around band-pass filters.

It is also good for thinning out sounds and can be used on percussive sounds as well as creating effects type of sounds.

I often get emails from programmers wanting to know how they can get that old radio effect or telephone line chat effect or even NASA space dialogue from space to Houston. Well, this is one of the tools. Use it and experiment.

Notch filter – also known as a band reject filter

The inverse of a band-pass is the notch filter. This is a very potent EQ/filter. It can home in on a single frequency band, and cut/boost it. Used specifically for 'problem' frequencies, the notch can be one of the most useful filters.

This is the exact opposite of the band-pass filter. It allows frequencies below and above the cut-off and attenuates the frequencies around the cut-off point.

In terms of the diagram shown for band-pass filtering, the area in between the two arrows is rejected (cut out), and the remaining frequencies below and above the cut-off are allowed to pass through. This is the exact opposite of band-pass filtering.

Why is this good? Well, it eliminates a narrow band of frequencies (the frequencies around the cut-off) – that in itself is a great tool. You can use this on all sounds and can have a distinct effect on a sound, not only in terms of eliminating the frequencies that you want eliminated, but also in terms of creating a new flavour to a sound.

But its real potency is in eliminating frequencies you don't want. Because when you select the cut-off point you are in essence selecting the frequencies around that cut-off point and eliminating them.

This is an invaluable tool when you want to hone in on a band of frequencies located, for example, right in the middle of a sound or recording. I sometimes use a notch filter on drum sounds that have a muddy or heavy mid section, or on sounds that have a little noise or frequency clash in the mid section of a sound.

Parametric

Invented by George Massenberg, this filter is one of the most commonly used today. This filter controls three parameters; frequency, bandwidth and gain. You select the range of frequencies you want to boost or cut, you select the width of that range and then use the gain to boost or cut the frequencies (within the selected bandwidth)d by a selected amount.

The frequencies not in the bandwidth are not altered. If you widen the band-width to the limit of the upper and lower frequencies ranges then this is called shelving. Most parametric filters have shelving parameters.

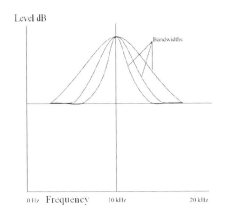

Figure 8.6
Parametric Filters

Parametric filters are great for more complex filtering jobs and can be used to create real dynamic effects because they can attenuate or boost any range of fre-quencies.

Basically, the parametric EQ places several active filters across the frequency spectrum. Each filter is designated to a frequency range; low, mid, high etc. You have the usual cut/boost, resonant frequency and bandwidth. It is these qualities and the control over them that places this particular EQ in the producer's arse-nal of dynamic tools. However, you need to understand what you are doing when using a parametric EQ, otherwise things can go very wrong.

Understand frequencies and sound, and you will be in total control.

Quasi-parametric EQ

This is just another form of parametric EQ but without the bandwidth control.

Sweep EQ

This is very similar to a band-pass filter, but with variable centre frequency, and no control over the width of the filter response (Q).

You will find that most mixers will have band-pass EQ, and some will have sweep EQ (where the centre frequency can be varied, also known as 'tuneable'), but very few, mainly digital, will have parametric EQ.

Paragraphic EQ

Another variation on the graphic EQ. This EQ provides control over the centre frequency of each band. Also regarded as a cross between the graphic and parametric EQs, this EQ offers multiple parametric peaking filters, where the gain of each is provided on a slider much like the graphic EQ.

Phase

We know that affecting the frequencies that we have chosen for equalization also affects the phase of those selected frequencies in relation to the unaffected frequencies. The process itself also affects the frequency response of the signal being treated. We are talking about tiny offsets here. Every time a frequency range is selected and treated, the affected frequencies will exhibit displacement in relation to the unaffected frequencies.

This offset is phase. We are not talking about big swirling phase effects here (as in guitar phasing) we are however talking about the pure definition of phase. This is probably not something that you will hear as phase, but it is something that affects our perception of the treated frequencies.

Why is this important?

This is what differentiates the tonal characteristics of analogue hardware and digital software EQs. The analogue EQ unit will exhibit far more musical phase changes than its digital counterpart, and at very low gains, whereas the digital EQ unit will have the advantage of leaving the phase relationships hardly affected, thus allowing for more robust gain changes.

It is true to state that all analogue, and almost all digital EQs, produce phase shifts when cutting *or* boosting. The filtering process used when conducting EQ tasks has a phase response which varies relative to the frequency. This process will impose a small 'delay' (offset) which creates the phase shift. These delays will vary according to frequency, the time factor in the delay itself, and whether you are boosting or cutting. The process of equalization alters the signal in terms of time and frequency.

Most analogue equalizers are 'minimum phase' designs (Butterworth designs), whereby some frequencies experience a different amount of 'processing' delay to others. The steeper the filter, the worse the phase-response variations become, which inherently distorts the waveform shape. This is referred to as phase distortion.

In contrast, a filter with a 'linear phase' response provides a constant time delay for all frequencies. It is also true to state that this 'delay' is equal whether cutting or boosting, so the argument of introducing phase when boosting is moot. However, phase does vary in terms of perception when using analogue versus digital. Analogue EQ phase can be far more 'musical', as the smearing process can be pleasing – much like harmonic distortion is when driving analogue consoles into their headroom. They both have their uses.

EQing kick drum

It is now time to begin with walk through examples. The following examples will deal with instruments and vocals; this way we have a good variety of scenarios to deal with, and a good range of frequencies to cover and manipulate.

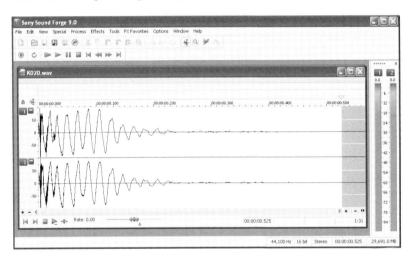

As you can see from Figure 10.1, I have opened up a kick file (filename K020) in Sound Forge. We are now going to manipulate this file and create new files by the simple use of EQ.

However, before we perform any type of manipulation, I want to show you how to evaluate and see the frequency spectrum (range) of any selected audio file. For this, we use a piece of software, or hardware, called a Spectrum Analyser. Sound Forge has this tool under the menu option, View - Spectrum Analyser. Figure 10.2 displays the frequency spectrum of the kick when played.

By using the analyser we are able to fully see the frequency start, the frequency body and the frequency tail-off. This type of tool is invaluable in helping us to apply EQ but do not rely on it solely, as most Spectrum Analysers come into their own in determining low-end frequencies, although they do cover the whole spectrum as can be seen in Figure 10.2.

You will appreciate how useful this tool is when we come to removing unwanted frequencies, or when we come to using EQ to either correct flawed vocals, or thin out or thicken vocal lines.

Figure 10.2
Spectrum Analysis of K020.wav

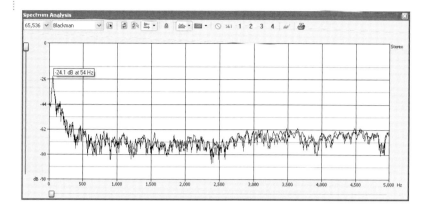

- The Y axis (left hand side figures) denotes amplitude/level in dB.
- The X axis (bottom figures) denotes the frequency in Hz.

The analyser tells us that this kick starts on a frequency of 0 Hz at – 60 dB (attack), rises to 54 Hz at -24 dB (height of attack's decay), drops and levels off. I have selected a range to be shown within the Spectrum Analyser's settings menu. In this instance I have selected a range not to exceed 5 kHz. Figure 10.3 shows us the full range from 20 Hz to 20 kHz.

Figure 10.3
Full Range Spectrum Analysis of K020.wav

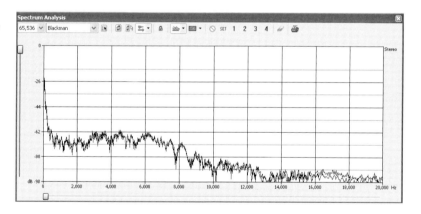

This helps us a great deal in understanding the characteristic and shape of the kick sound, and this in turn gives us a numerical and graphical reference for setting up our EQ parameters. However, as stated earlier, use the Spectrum Analyser purely as a guide.

What did I just say, in English? Simple: check the same image but zoomed in (Figure 10.4). Sound Forge has a great tool for zooming in a range of frequencies by simply dragging the cursor from the start of the range to the end of the range. This allows us to view the frequencies in closer detail.

I highlighted the peak of the kick file's waveform with the mouse and it gave me the figure above. I can move my mouse over any part of the waveform and it will highlight the data I need. With this example, I can now decide what type of EQ I want to apply and by how much.

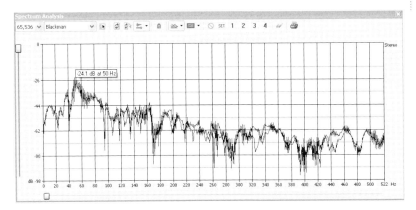

Figure 10.4
Zoomed Spectrum Analysis of k020.wav

The punch component, or attack, of most kick drums lies between about 40 and 110Hz. This is where you find the low-end energy of most kicks. Below this range you'll mostly feel rather than hear any boost. It's easy to either neglect this and be left with all sorts of low frequency imbalances in your mix, or to be confused by what is actually the 'bottom-end' of your mix.

However, when using EQ to filter the lower end of, say, a kick drum in a mix context, it is imperative to analyse *all* the low-end energy which could be summed by using the kick, bass, low pads etc.

With sounds that tend to be 'warmer', as opposed to 'cutting', you will invariably find that the frequency area concentrated on is between 180 – 220 Hz. Working on a kick that might need to be more prominent in the mix, or cut through on mid-range monitors, the 2 – 6 kHz range is where the manipulation takes place.

Graphic EQ

From the Soundforge menu option, I am going to choose a graphic EQ (Process > EQ > Graphic). I have not input or drawn in the EQ curve. The Graphic EQ is currently at default with all the parameters at 0. Now, let us shape the EQ curve by using the nodes in the Graphic EQ window.

The default line (middle of screen) is at 0dB, across the whole frequency spectrum. By placing the mouse over any part of the line, I can create a 'node' and then move this node. I can keep on creating nodes, so that I have control over the default line. The more nodes, the more detailed your control over the shape (response).

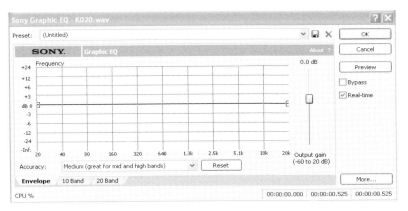

Figure 10.5
Graphic EQ

Figure 10.6
EQ Nodes in Soundforge

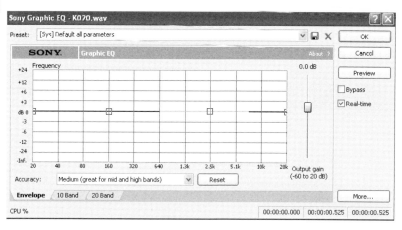

I have always preferred visual interfaces for these types of dynamic manipulations as opposed to inputting fields and numerical data into graphs. I can visually create the EQ curves here, instead of having to input numbers and hope for the best. There is also something very satisfying in having such instant and visual control.

Earlier we talked about graphic EQs having fixed bands and that you could only apply boost or cut to these bands. But Sound Forge has given us variable and adjustable frequency bands and these are selected and determined via the nodes. Figure 10.6 shows what I mean by nodes. As you can see, I have a total of four nodes (little boxes) across the default line which I have created. I am now going to move these nodes around and create an EQ shape for the kick drum file (Figure 10.7).

Figure 10.7
Using nodes to create EQ shape

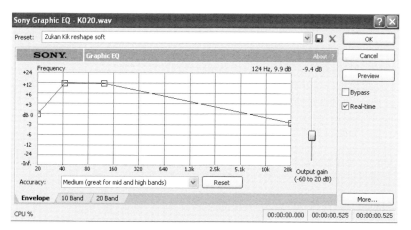

When boosting frequencies always make sure not to clip the file (i.e. don't go beyond 0 dBFS). Make sure to compensate for any boosts. I have adjusted the output gain to –9.4 dB so as to compensate the huge boost of 12 dB on the kick sample.

Usually, I would not generate such huge boost values, but for the purposes of this tutorial I chose to make sure the processes are clearly visible and audible. The 'shape' of the frequency curve shows that I have eaten into the attack of the

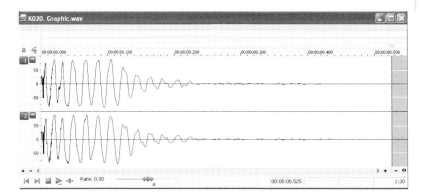

Figure 10.8
K020 with graphic EQ applied

Sound file

K020_graphic.wav

Info

All the sound files referred to in this book can be downloaded from:

www.pc-publishing.com/soundeq.html

kick sample by moving the second node away from 0. This can easily be heard when listening to the processed file.

By a simple four node process I have created a new sonic texture by using the same sample. And once you press 'OK', that will render the new EQ shape over the audio file. The result is shown in Figure 10.8.

The kick file now sounds deeper, with less 'top-end'. The EQ shape accents the attack and decay of the attack, and drops rapidly from there, thus making the body and tail seem both quieter and as if the higher frequencies have been filtered (which they have).

Now let us put this file into the Spectrum Analyser. This will show if I am right or wrong (Figure 10.9).

Yep, spot on. You can see that the attack and attack decay are peaked and

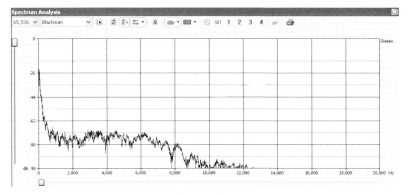

Figure 10.9
Spectrum Analysis of K020 after graphic EQ

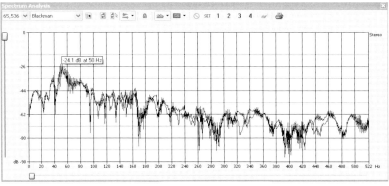

Figure 10.10
Zoomed version of Figure 10.9

smoothed between 50 Hz – 66 Hz. After that, the amplitude drops dramatically over the frequency spectrum.

Have fun with the Spectrum Analyser feature in your audio editor - you will be amazed at how much you will learn, just by viewing frequency spectrums of different audio files.

Paragraphic EQ

Now let us use the same kick file, but with a different type of EQ, an EQ we discussed earlier - the Paragraphic EQ. So, to begin, we perform the exact same sequence as before. In fact, it is good practice to stick to a procedure and to keep practicing that. This helps you to perform tasks quicker and to fault find in the event that you have made a mistake in the process.

Load the paragraphic EQ via the Soudforge menu option: Process > EQ >Paragraphic. Figure 10.11 shows the parameters of the paragraphic EQ. There

Figure 10.11
Paragraphic EQ

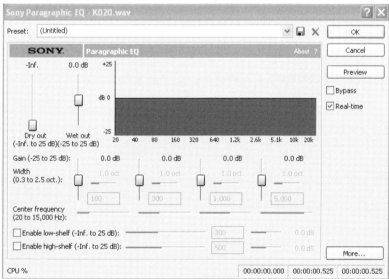

are four bands and each bandwidth can be adjusted. This paragraphic EQ has a little more control than the usual paragraphic EQs, in that you can not only shape the bands by adjusting the centre frequencies and their amounts, but also vary the position of each band. You also have the options of choosing low or hi-shelf filtering.

In Figure 10.12, I have chosen to create a much thinner and crisper sound. By removing the 'body' of the sample and boosting the higher frequencies, the sound is now far more pronounced and thinner sounding. Basically, I have left the attack portion of the sample intact but removed the fuller frequencies that follow. I have then boosted the upper mid to higher frequencies. This is a good way of explaining how to use this EQ and how it sounds.

Figure 10.13 shows the new kick file after being rendered with the paragraphic EQ. This new kick waveform shows what the paragraphic EQ has done to the frequency and amplitude of the waveform.

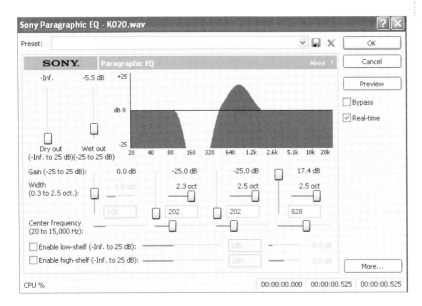

Figure 10.12
Paragraphic EQ on soundfile K020

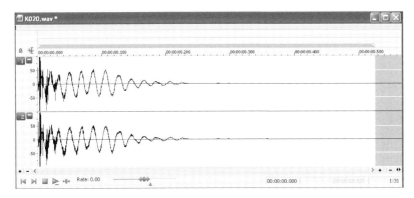

Figure 10.13
K020 waveform after rendering with
Paragraphic EQ

Sound file

K020 Paragraphic mid to top.wav

Corrective use of paragraphic EQ

The paragraphic EQ can be used very effectively as a Notch Filter (Figure 10.14) and also to demonstrate the Fletcher Munson Curve (Figure 10.16).

Figure 10.14 shows how to use the Paragraphic EQ as a Notch Filter to isolate and remove 60 Hz cycle hum. This is a great tool to have as there are times when your audio file might exhibit mains hum at 60 Hz. This way you can isolate and remove the hum.

You can select to notch out any range of frequencies as shown in Figure 10.15. Here, all four bands have been selected for notch treatment. Of course, you would almost never use any more than a single band at a time, as multi-notched bands can alter a sound dramatically. Notch EQ is very useful for the removal of 'problem' frequencies as discussed earlier. But, as with most processes, experiment and have fun and gauge for yourself the impact of the process on the sound.

Info

All the sound files referred to in this book can be downloaded from:

www.pc-publishing.com/soundeq.html

Figure 10.14
Paragraphic as a Notch Filter

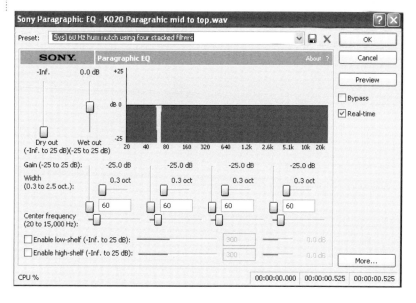

Figure 10.15
60Hz hum 4 way notch

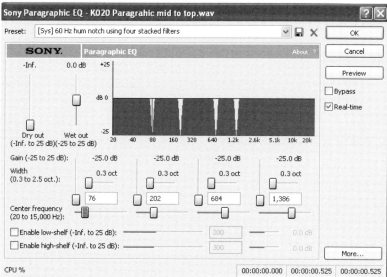

In this instance, EQ is used to cut and boost selected frequencies, so that a more balanced gain structure is kept right throughout the hearing spectrum at low listening levels. The Fletcher Munson Curve is far more apt on entire mixes than on single isolated sounds.

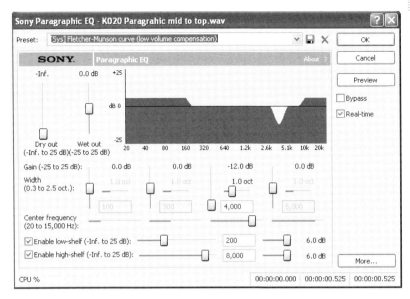

Figure 10.16
Fletcher-Munson Curve

Now let us use the same kick file, but this time we will use a Parametric EQ. I like using this EQ, because not only is it simple to use, but it also has additional filter settings that make this EQ very versatile.

Look at the settings I am using in Figure 10.17. I have adjusted the parameters so that I am left with a high frequency shelf. I am actually cutting frequencies and not boosting. The kick file I am using for these examples is a good all round kick file that covers most of the frequencies I would expect to see in a file of this nature, and is not limited to any particular frequency. That is why it is such a good file to use.

As we discussed earlier, cutting is always preferred to boosting, and this example reflects that thinking beautifully.

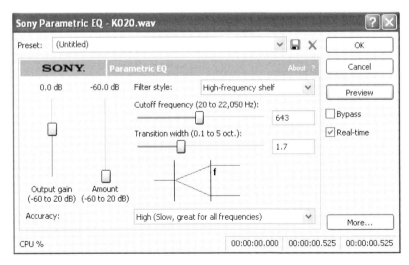

Figure 10.17
Paragraphic EQ

Sound file

K020 Parametric high shelf.wav1

The sample now sounds far more rounded, deeper and 'woollen'. By removing hi-range frequencies we are left with the full attack and body. As mentioned earlier, cutting has a direct impact on unaltered frequencies. In this case cutting the higher frequencies pronounces the lower frequencies more.

And now I have used the Band-pass Filter on the Parametric, to give the kick sound a boxy feel (Figure 10.18).

Figure 10.18
60Hz hum 4 way notch

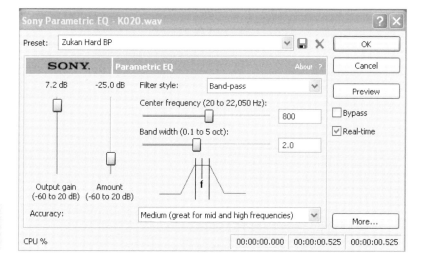

Sound file

K020 Parametric boxy.wav1

By selecting the filter style (better to be named as type) as Band-Pass with a filter frequency of 800 Hz and a 2 octave bandwidth I am able to create a 'boxy' sounding effect. This filter type is also the one that is most commonly used when creating the 'telephone' effect on vocals (we will come to this later).

Figure 10.19 is an image of a 2 band EQ, as discussed earlier and is probably the simplest of all EQs to use.

Figure 10.19
2 Band EQ

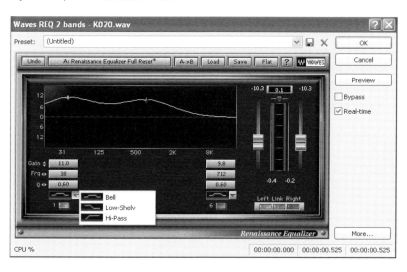

Sound file

K020 2 band EQ.wav

As you can see, you have only two nodes to play with. This EQ is really self explanatory. For four bands of EQ, simply add another two bands to the above. The thinking is the same.

I have selected the Bell shape for filter response as I do not want to apply any hi or low shelving. The Bell shape also allows for a more gradual rise and drops for the peak, being asymmetrical in that it has symmetrical response characteristics irrespective of whether I cut or boost. In this instance the EQ process is more subtle and fluid.

Although I have used boosts as opposed to cuts you can hear that the effect is quite subtle but clear. By boosting at 38 Hz and shaping the ensuing frequencies, I am able to apply a smooth curve for the attack which is clearly evident when listening to the rendered file. The attack does not possess that harshness that was evident and the body sounds a little more rounded as I have applied another boost at 712 Hz.

Figure 10.20 shows what happens when you alter the filter types to low shelf and low-pass.

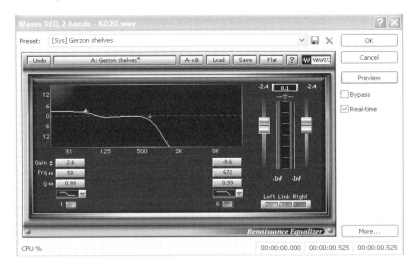

Figure 10.20
2 Band with low shelf and low pass

I have adjusted the two nodes at 58 Hz and 672 Hz and selected low shelf and low-pass from the drop down menus below the parameter settings. The drum sounds far more muffled and darker. It is vibrant in low frequencies with almost no high frequencies to balance out the sound. This is very useful when trying to attain the deeper and darker type of drum sounds.

Drums are probably the easiest instruments to EQ. The real art of kick drum EQ is to consider the bass line sound in the song that the drums reside in. As they invariably share similar frequency ranges, they must be processed with care and attention.

Apply small amounts of EQ, as the process and result of applying any dynamics will result in some form of degradation. So, be sensible and wary of drastic changes. Keep things natural.

Separation also comes into the equation; the whole 'drive' of modern Hip Hop and Dance songs are centred round the marriage between the kick drum and the bass line.

EQing snare drum

As there are so many types of snares, trying to classify them in one specific frequency band would be impossible; however, the low-end (or fatness) of snares generally lies in the 100-440 Hz frequency range. The energy of the snare's body will tend to be in the 750-1.4 kHz frequency range and the crispness of the attack will lie in the 4-8 kHz frequency range.

These are generalizations, but they will give you an idea as to where you might want to begin, when applying EQ. But, as with all these examples, the Spectrum Analyser is your best friend.

With EQ it is often very easy to create a varied selection of snares from one source snare. Let us begin with a simple snare sound (Figure 11.1).

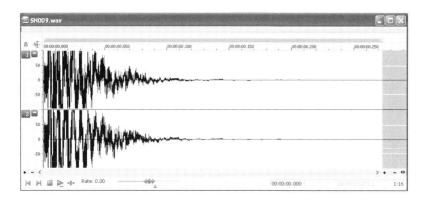

Figure 11.1
Snare (SN009)

This is a standard mid-range bucket snare, comprising a metallic base with some noise element. Generally, a good Hip Hop snare sound. Now let us create another snare from this source snare.

4 band Paragraphic EQ

I am going to use a 4 band Paragraphic EQ, but this time I am going to select the type of band I want to adopt. With certain software/hardware dynamics, you have the facility to select the filter shape (or EQ shape) of the band. In this instance I am using the Bell shape. You can see from Figure 11.2 that I have selected the Bell shape for three of the bands. The Bell simply denotes the shape of the frequency curve (as discussed earlier) and offers a more gradual rise and drop to the peak.

Figure 11.2
4 Band Paragraphic

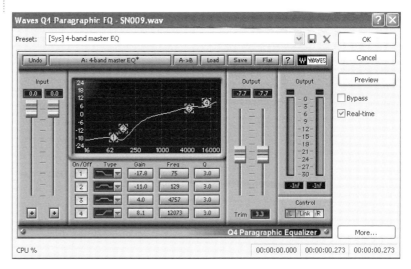

With the settings I have used above, I have concentrated more on the mid-range frequencies of the snare sound. This is a good way to remove the low-end frequencies and keep the mid-range 'alive', and the top-end as is. You can clearly see what frequency bands I have used and by how much.

This EQ allows me to move the bands via the numbered nodes. I can also turn off any nodes that I do not want to use. I can also change the shape of the bands too (Figure 11.3). This gives me more flexibility and choice, and editing this way is so much easier and instant.

Figure 11.3
Different Shape Bands

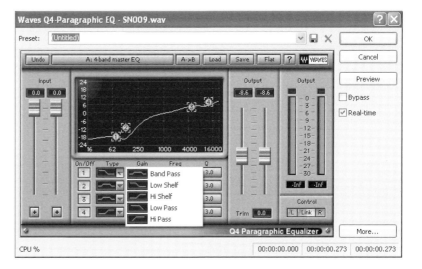

Figure 11.4 shows the result, after rendering the original snare with the EQ.

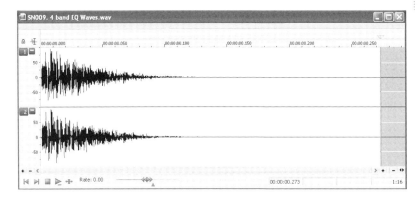

Figure 11.4
SN009 after EQ

Sound file

SN009 4 band EQ Waves.wav

5 band EQ

In Figure 11.5, I have selected a 5 band EQ. As you can see, I can change the EQ shapes for each band, but I also have Resonance and Q for the filter types. If you are having problems understanding the above, then go back to Chapter 8 where Resonance and Q are explained.

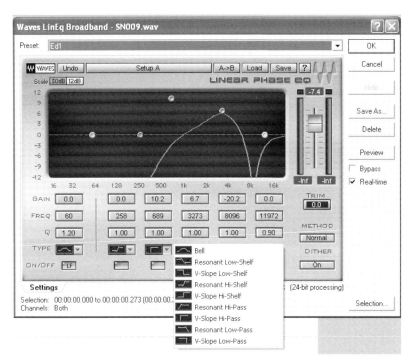

Figure 11.5
5 Band Linear EQ

Sound file

SN009 with Linear EQ.wav

Info

All the sound files referred to in this book can be downloaded from:

www.pc-publishing.com/soundeq.html

I like this EQ a lot as it allows me far more detail and control over the frequency bands. I also have a main out for the bands, with its own parameters; frequency shape, resonance, Q, low-pass filter and overall gain.

Just for fun, I created a crazy shape for the bands, but it really sounds tight and painful. This EQ will give you endless hours of fun and is one of the most detailed of the EQ plug-ins available.

I could go on and on with examples of snare EQ, but I feel that you have enough information above to start to try some of your own EQ projects. As mentioned earlier, and many times, keep it simple and do not apply too much EQ unless you are after a certain effect.

I picked kicks and snares as my subject matter here, simply because they are the most common percussive sounds that get treated with EQ. It would be pointless to repeat the above for claps, hi hats, or any other percussive sound, as you have more than enough information to help you to apply these techniques to any percussive element. If you do have any problems with frequency ranges, just use the Spectrum Analyser, but more importantly your ears.

Let your ears be the most potent and trustworthy tools at your disposal.

EQing drum loops

Drum loops are a little more complex, as the loop itself might incorporate a number of percussive sounds that all need to be considered when EQ is applied. However, this is not as complicated as it seems.

The trick here is to try to make sure that you treat each drum sound separately, with the final stereo mix of the drum loop incorporating varying EQ curves for the isolated drum sounds.

I find that using the same EQ software/hardware for all the individual drum sounds makes the final loop sound more natural. As mentioned earlier, different EQ units have different tonal qualities, so keeping to the same unit makes the process sound more natural.

There is nothing worse than hearing an acoustic loop that houses drum sounds that sound as if they are from different kits. There are times when using different samples from different sources are needed, particularly in the Dance and Hip Hop genres, but in terms of using EQ to shape the sounds it is important to think about how they need to be presented to the listener. Using complementary sounds always works well as the ear and brain immediately recognise the similarities and treat them as aesthetic, as opposed to trying to make sense of alienated sounds.

Keep it simple, keep it safe. For this to happen, you will need all the drum components in separate tracks, and instances of the same EQ used on each track. If however, all you are presented with is a stereo file of the drum loop with no individual tracks of the drum components, then you need to consider the whole frequency range of the entire drum loop when using EQ.

Always be aware of what it is that you are applying EQ to. You need to make sure that the treated sound has a natural finish to it.

With drum loops you need to think ahead, and even more importantly, to be aware of what other sounds will be used with the loop. If the drum loop sounds a bit thin, don't despair, the bass sound might compensate.

In other words, unless you are after a specific effect, the drums must always have a good dynamic frequency range, with flowing frequencies, as opposed to a compacted frequency range (narrow banded). This will ensure a lively drum loop with all the components nicely residing in their frequency ranges. A narrow banded (narrow bandwidth) drum loop will always sound thin and exhausting. The more variety and richness in the frequencies selected the more the ear and brain keeps interested.

Used gently and intelligently, EQ can dynamically change a drum loop's sound but maintain the believable and natural dynamic frequency content inherent in the individual components of the drum loop. Another area to be very wary of is that of frequency crossovers (overlaps). For example, the high-end of a snare sound might start to share the low-end frequencies of a hi hat sound, the mid-range of a kick might share frequencies with the low-end of a tom drum, or vice versa.

Always be cautious of these frequency overlaps, otherwise there will be gain boosts where frequencies overlap, plus possible phasing issues and a host of other anomalies.

Let me explain the above with examples. First off, we will use a simple drum loop and apply EQ to give varying versions of the same loop. Figure 12.1 is a straightforward drum loop incorporating a kick, snare and hi hats.

Figure 12.1
'Beat 1 90bpm.wav' – a simple drum loop.

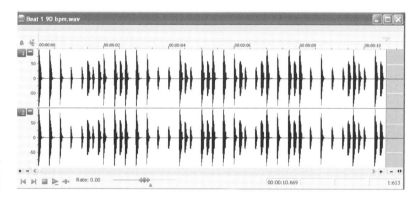

Sound file

Beat 1 90 BPM.wav

5 band Linear Broadband

Now let us EQ it. I am using the same EQ as I used earlier, the 5 band Linear Broadband. Figure 12.2 shows what I have done with regards to shaping the EQ curves. I have gone for a drastic separation effect.

The drums now sound more separated and crispier, slightly dirtier, but louder. This is not subtle, but I have deliberately done this so you can fully appreciate what we can do with EQ

Figure 12.2
Drum loop with added 5 Band Linear EQ

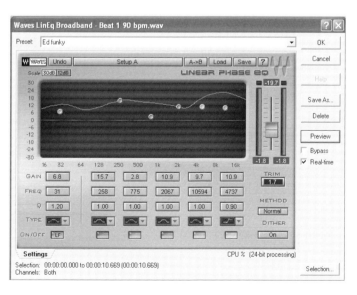

Sound file

Beat 1 after Linear EQ.wav

10 band Paragraphic EQ

In this next example (Figure 12.3), I am going to show you how to fill up the frequency 'space' of the loop (the area across the whole frequency spectrum) and mimic 'stereo spread'. I am using a 10-band Paragraphic EQ. I need loads of bands so I can have greater control over all the individual frequency bands. As you can see from the image, the EQ also offers me all the usual band shape options.

What am I trying to achieve here? I am trying to create what we call 'Pseudo Stereo'. Pseudo Stereo usually means creating a stereo effect using a filter or dynamics. In this instance, we are using EQ to create a stereo effect.

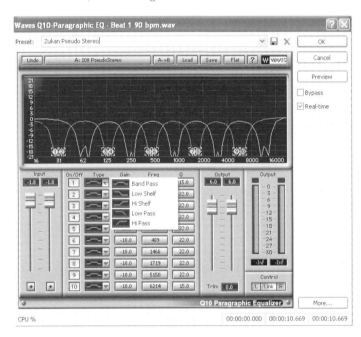

Figure 12.3
10 Band Paragraphic applied

Sound file

Beat 1 10 Band Para.wav

This is quite an extreme example and, as you can hear, it is not perfectly balanced across the axis. This is more to do with the way the loop was constructed with the hi hats being panned just off centre. However, I have deliberately made it extreme so you can see all the band points and how they affect the audio.

While we are using the 10 band Paragraphic EQ it might be worthwhile to show you how to create the 'telephone' effect using 6 of the 10 bands. The idea behind the telephone effect is to work on the mid-range frequencies and narrow band them with extreme hi-pass filtering at the low to low mid-range, and low-pass filtering at the hi-mid to hi-range frequencies. This is clearly demonstrated in Figure 12.4.

You will notice that apart from the first node, I have selected a combination of hi-pass filtering (filter type) at the lower ranges and low-pass filtering at the higher ranges.

Of course, you do not need so many bands when dealing with a single drum loop that is not too varied in its frequency content. But for the sake of this tutorial, I thought it best to show you how you can use most types of EQ to attain the same results.

Figure 12.4
Telephone effect

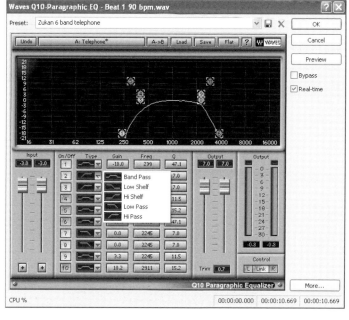

Beat 1 Telephone effect.wav

6 band EQ

This next example (Figure 12.5) is a template I have created using a 6 band EQ with more parameters for 'Peak' and 'Shelving'. The parameters are extreme and actually off the chart. I can't even see the nodes. Why have I created this template? I have created this for drum layering purposes.

All these software based EQ units allow for saving your own EQ edits. It is a good policy to save every template you create. Calling up templates for any given project

Figure 12.5
EQ Template (Shelf Bass Tilt)

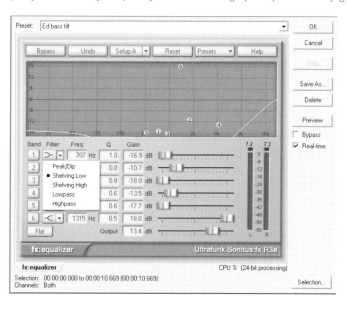

Sound file

Beat 1 shelf bass tilt.wav

makes life so much easier and saves you loads of hard work trying to replicate a template that you created but have since lost. Imagine if you had created the greatest of all EQ templates, but didn't save it? It would make a grown man weep.

Now listen to the sample and evaluate what is happening. I often create beat templates for my drum layering tasks as it makes for a great library to dip into when needed. This particular loop exhibits a soft yet pronounced hi-end and a warmer but relatively thin low-end. This makes for a great loop that can be lay-

Figure 12.6
Layered Loops

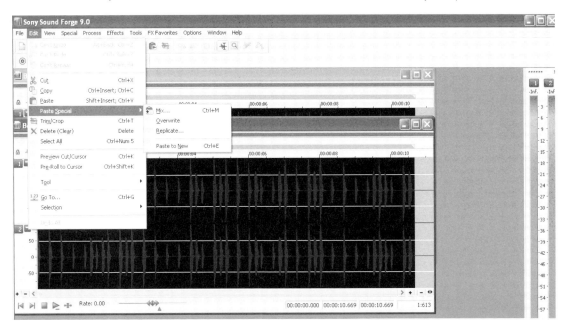

ered with another drum loop. The two together will make a really deep and crisp loop. In fact I have done exactly this in Figure 12.6. I have layered the original drum loop with the processed 'bass tilt' one.

I have layered the two drum loops by using one of Sound Forge's paste tools, available from: Menu > Edit > Paste Special > Mix.

You can also do the exact opposite, creating a beat that is rich in mid to high frequencies, and then layer that with a deeper low-end beat. You can even play your own drum sounds over the beat and create a new beat. It is endless. You are only limited by your imagination, and not by the tools.

We will now run through an example incorporating a drum beat with all the individual components on separate tracks in a software sequencer. Figure 12.7 shows three track instances of audio, recorded in Cubase. The tracks are broken into the following drum sounds: snare, kick and shaker.

This is a very simple drum beat, and it will serve our purpose perfectly. I have opened three instances of EQ, one on each channel. The EQ units that I am using are the standard default 4-band EQ provided with the software.

Sound file

Beat 1 layered with shelf.wav

Sound file

The Beat EQs.wav

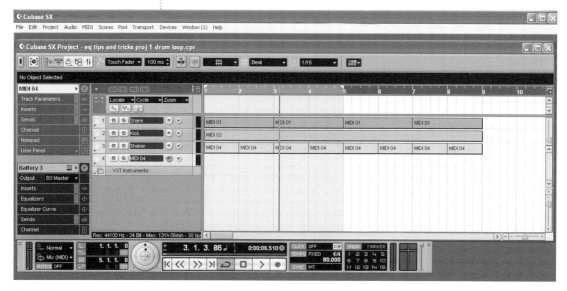

Figure 12.7
Cubase Project, multi-track recording of individual drum tracks

I have treated the snare to be a little harsh and dirty, with a lot of mid to top-end. The kick has been treated to make it thumping and pronounced in the low to mid-end. The shakers have been treated to be a little on the mid-end, so as to complement the frequency gap between the kick and snare (Figure 12.8).

The 4 nodes, one for each band, are clearly evident in this image. This is the EQ unit used for the shaker. You can see that I have boosted the mid to high frequencies in a gentle manner, but with incrementing values.

Figure 12.8
Shaker EQ

Sound file

Shaker EQ.wav

You must always be very aware of the frequency ranges that you are boosting or cutting. Keep checking all the EQ settings and make sure there are very few overlaps, if any. As the image shows I am playing and adjusting to taste (metering shows this) and although in this instance the shaker is soloed, I will always EQ whilst playing the whole drum beat or mix if other elements are involved.

I have deliberately used this type of EQ curve for the shaker, because I know that I will be treating the kick with more emphasis in the low to mid-end, and the snare with emphasis in the mid to top-end. This method affords me a good frequency spread across the whole spectrum. If there are serious overlaps in the EQ curves, then the file will suffer.

The only time I deliberately overlap frequencies is when I am after a very specific effect. An example would be boosting the mid-range of a drum loop so as to fit the bass line in its own space. In this instance I would overlap the kick and snare frequencies and boost the shared frequency range, and then lower the gain so as not to cause any tonal anomalies like distortion, clipping etc.

You can see the shape of the EQ is tailing off towards the mid-end but the attack and decay of the attack have been boosted. I have boosted at 200 Hz with a small

Figure 12.9
Kick EQ Treatment

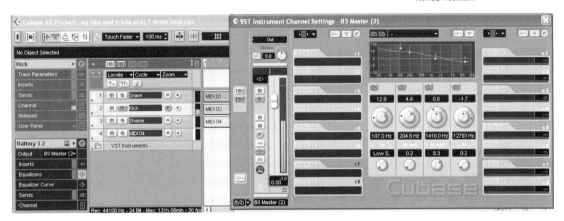

gain of 4 dB, and then tailed it off towards the higher end frequencies. I did this so as to create a thick, low-end boom. Once we shape the snare frequencies you will hear how the three elements combine to form a strong yet balanced sonic texture. Again, you can always change the shapes of any of the EQ units.

The whole point of this exercise to show you how to sensibly select EQ parameters and make full use of the frequency bands available. Bear in mind that we have the option to turn off any of the bands in this example. This allows us to use the EQ unit as a 'one band eq', all the way up to four bands.

Sound file

Kick EQ.wav

Figure 12.10
EQ curve for the snare sound

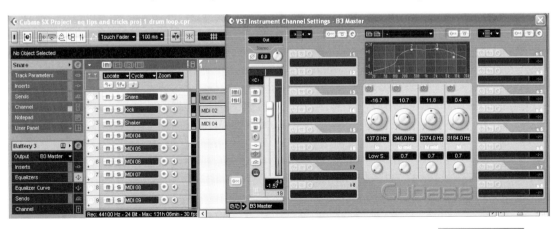

As you can see, I have shaped quite a pronounced curve for the snare EQ. I have heavily boosted from around 340 Hz onwards with a gentle drop back down to 0 after the main mid to hi-mid. This has made the snare a little grainy and yet very snappy, as there is a lot of very high boosted gains across the mid-range (energy).

Sound file

Snare EQ.wav

Now listen to the finalised file:

You can hear the differences from the 'dry' (untreated) and the 'wet' (treated) files. It is clearly evident that the original beat has undergone some very serious treatment. I have, of course, used extreme curves so as to show you how to get variety and new sonic textures from the same elements.

EQ curves for all three drum tracks

To conclude this section, take a look at the EQ curves of all three drum sounds in Figure 12.11, and you will notice that combined, they form a half decent EQ curve with emphasis across most of the frequency ranges. Take note of where I have cut and where I have boosted.

Figure 12.11
EQ curves for all three drum tracks.

Let us now process the original beat with a couple of manic variations that normally I would not advise. But you can get extremely creative with EQ and use it to accentuate any frequency spectrum.

Figure 12.12 shows an extreme and contorted curve that I have created by using 4 bands. By selecting a low-shelf curve for the first node, bell shapes for the next two and a hi-shelf for the last node, I am able to accent the low and high

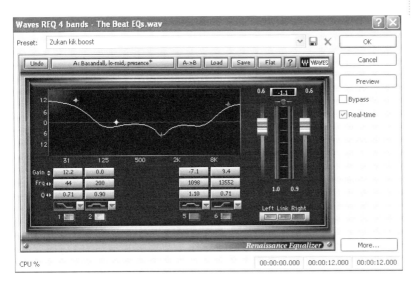

Figure 12.12
Extreme 4 Band EQ.

Sound file

The beat contorted.wav.

frequency ranges by attenuating the frequencies I do not want exposed. Because I am using shelves, I am allowing the response to extend beyond the selected frequency to it's highest or lowest range value. By using a low-shelf I am able to allow all the frequencies to pass through from my selected frequency to the lowest value. The shape of the filter type denotes what it does.

I have applied a huge boost to frequencies between 44 and 200 Hz and by selecting the low-shelf filter I am able to shape the response of the low frequencies all the way from the selected frequency to its lowest limit. The opposite applies when using a hi-shelf.

The fact that there is a Q function means that the filters can be resonant. We can thank Michael Gerzon for introducing us to resonant shelf filters. The higher the Q value, the steeper the slope and thus more resonance. Values below 1.00 offer a more gentle slope and are therefore far more usable for general applications. You can use higher Q values when you want to home in and treat a very narrow frequency range with minimal affect on other frequencies.

But the Q can be used for creative purposes too. It is important to understand that the Q value functions differently for each filter type.

- Bell - Q corresponds to the width of the frequency range for that band as explained earlier.
- Shelf - Q controls the slope of the shelf and therefore the resonant dips and peaks.
- Cut - Q controls the slope of the cut filter.

I will give one more example of EQ mangling for the drum loop. Figure 12.13 shows what can be achieved when using the right types of filters. You should be able to work out by now why I have used a hi-shelf for the lower frequencies and Bell shapes for the remaining three bands.

Figure 12.13
Further EQ mangling.

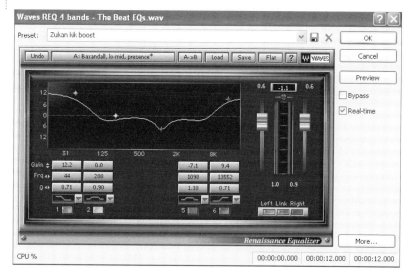

The beat contorted 2.wav.

This beat now has far less low-end energy, a subdued mid and a topped hi-end. The beat itself sounds far more 'narrow banded' around the mid and high frequencies and imparts a 'boxy' type of character. This is a great way of thinning certain frequencies to accommodate room for other frequencies.

I selected to create an extreme curve so as to display how easy it is to shape a sound by simply using the right type of filter curves and applying them with an understanding of what the result will sound like. I hope these 'extremes' have been of use to you.

The time has come for us to move onto the most confusing and difficult of all sounds to treat, The Voice.

EQing voice

This is *the* area that most people have trouble with when it comes to using EQ.

For some strange reason, even engineers have to ponder a solution to an EQ problem where the voice is concerned. I always have to think through the whole process; taking into account the desired result, the choice of EQ to use, the corrective and creative approaches, and all this married with what my client requires for the market that the mix is aimed at. Maybe not that strange when you take into account the vast frequency range of the voice, coupled with the varying fluctuations (gains) of frequencies over a given length of time.

Add to that the usual problems encountered in recording the voice, like plosives and pops, and you can see that half the time engineers are applying Corrective EQ, as opposed to Creative EQ.

And if that wasn't enough, singers then go and change the gains across their vocals and fluctuate the frequencies even further by applying vibrato to their voice whilst singing, and it is now even clearer as to why this area of EQ treatment is regarded as the 'Holy Grail'.

Whereas drum sounds are one shot and static, in terms of their frequency ranges the voice encompasses a whole plethora (love that word) of frequencies and at varying amplitudes over a given period. And it does not end there, oh no. You need to take into account the frequency ranges of the instruments incorporated within a mix, and compensate for that, as well as trying to line up the voice in the mix.

If all the elements of a mix were static in their frequency ranges, then it would be easy. But since music is not like that, we have the problem of finding a happy location for each and every instrument and the voice. Now, if the voice has a habit of varying its frequencies, then it will 'invade' the spaces allocated to instruments. We will be left with frequency overlaps, clashes, phase, etc. So, the task of 'fitting' the vocal into a mix becomes more complex.

Multiple voices

Now, let's take that a stage further and introduce what really takes place in the real world, multiple voices. A song will invariably have more than one vocal, irrespective of there being only one vocalist. For example, choruses will entail more than one vocalist, or more than one vocal line. In other words, apart from having another vocalist singing on the song, you will have a number of vocal lines from one singer, or more, that will go to form the chorus or any other part of the song. And it doesn't end there: most vocals nowadays are double tracked, doubled up for thickness, layered to create harmonies and so on. Add to that the changes in the tonal character of the way the song is sung, and you are faced with even more variables to take into account.

Ok, so the above sounds as if you are going to go through a living hell when trying to EQ vocals but fear not, it is not that bleak. As we have covered earlier, there are ways to analyse the frequency range (spectrum) of any sound, be it an instrument or a voice. The methodology is the same. The Spectrum Analyser is a useful tool, so use it. But remember, your ears are the best tools available. The trick in applying EQ to vocals is to assess what the rest of the audio is doing around the vocals. Your primary concern with any song (and mix) is to place the processing focus on the vocals, because without the vocals you do not have a song.

I often enrich the frequencies around the vocals and then place the vocals in a central frequency band, smack bang in the middle of the mix with careful consideration for additional vocal lines be it backing vocals, secondary vocal hooks etc. Additionally, and crucially, I have to consider the vocals' frequency ranges so as to accommodate them with treatment to the surrounding frequencies.

This works well for some dance based music, but not for R&B. In dance music, I like the vocals to stay rigid in its frequency 'home', and let the music bounce around it, with vocal harmonies accenting the overall feel of the song, as opposed to dominating it like in R&B.

With R&B, I do the exact opposite, as the vocals are far more dynamic and flowing, so require a far broader frequency range to move in. In fact most R&B and current Hip Hop songs carry an abundance of vocal frequencies with multi layering harmonies, panned double tracking, and so on. On top of all this we have some very dynamically sung vocals that also enter the 'instrument' area, whereby the voice is used as an additional instrument: high-end falsettos that merge with high-end instrument sounds comes to mind.

Separation and layering

We also need to consider separation and layering with vocal lines when we talk about EQ. Considering not only the overall frequency ranges of all the vocals, but that of all sounds within a mix, will go a long way in resolving any frequency anomalies like masking, clashing etc. Separation is a crucial element of a mix, particularly with today's plethora of multi sound mixes. Cluttered mixes often fail at the first hurdle as they do not offer enough space and depth for the listener to evaluate the sonic content in a pleasing way. Instead they confuse the ear and brain, and end up simply being irritating.

The same applies to sparse mixes albeit in a different context. A sparse mix will require a great deal of depth and width with sensible frequency crossover points whereby huge gaps of empty space are not left in between the sounds. Sometimes filling out a sparse mix can be even harder than treating a cluttered mix.

Separation is also crucial when it comes to vocals, as the small nuances of the vocal delivery require that the whole transient nature of the sound be heard. Words, letters, sustained notes etc must all be distinct and heard with clarity and depth. The same can be said for all the musical components within a mix.

As we discussed earlier, EQ is a great tool to use if you need to separate instruments and vocals in a mix, but we didn't really touch on using EQ when we layer sounds, specifically vocals. Before we get our teeth into some vocal EQ examples, I would like to briefly touch on the subject of Primary and Secondary EQ.

Primary and secondary EQ

I have come across a number of producers who, like myself, like to EQ the vocals *without* the music, and then place it in the mix at the time of mixing/production. There is a vein of thought here that could be summed as 'clever'.

The idea behind this thinking is to get the vocals as clean and as dynamically strong as possible, prior to introducing it into the mix. This will then afford a clear idea as to where the vocals sit with respect to the other elements in the mix. This works quite well, and is a method with merit.

This is more about corrective EQ than creative EQ as the vocals need to be 'treated' as opposed to 'coloured' within a mix context. This will come later. This also gives the advantage of spotting any anomalies that may exist in the vocal files, be it; noise, hiss, poor microphone technique, plosives, pops etc.

With Primary EQ, you EQ the sound to make sure it is clean and dynamically strong, *prior* to placing it in the mix. This type of EQ does not entail colouring the sound, only making sure it is clean and neutral in terms of frequencies.

I adopt this method for additional reasons. By only dealing with the vocal files, I can examine the details that are crucial for a good production. Most notable is 'noise'. It is far easier to isolate and eradicate noise from the vocals if the vocals are on their own, with no other audio interfering with it. It is also much easier to isolate pops and plosives, and any anomaly, if the vocals are not being listened to in a mix of other sounds. Finally, it is easier to analyse the frequencies inherent in the vocal files, if isolated.

If you try to perform any of the above *within* a mix, then you will not be as successful or as accurate as adopting the isolation technique described above. Once you have clean and dynamic vocals, the mix will build around them far more accurately. By preparing your vocals prior to any mixing, you will give yourself the luxury of easier fault finding and allow yourself to be more creative.

Let me explain what I mean by fault finding. You will often encounter rogue frequencies in your mix. Something just doesn't sit right. But trying to find the 'problem' could take ages and cause you nightmares if there are other 'interfering' frequencies within the mix. If you *know* your vocals are good, then you can look elsewhere for the problem. A problem frequency on an instrument sound is always much easier to locate and fix. A problem frequency within the vocals could take far longer to isolate and repair.

Once the above has been accomplished, Secondary EQ can be applied. This entails treating the sound with EQ to make it 'fit' in the mix and can either be complemented or be complementary. This could involve:

- using 'coloured' EQs for adding that extra texture
- dynamically and creatively treating the vocals to fit in with the genre the mix is aimed at
- enhancing certain frequencies at certain parts of the song for effect
- using EQ to create layered effects (phase)

And so on. The Secondary EQ is about creativity and adaptation (genre and market relevant) and not about correction.

Voice examples

In production, we adopt a number of tricks to enhance and invigorate the mix. Most notable of these is layering vocals. This basically means that we take one vocal line, copy it and then treat it, and use it alongside the original vocal line. We could also double track vocals (recording the same vocal twice) and treat each vocal take separately or in unison. I will often take multi copies of the same vocal line and pan them and treat them in isolation, but audition in unison (listen to them all together) to get the optimum result. Of course, when dealing with the same copies of a file and then processing them with EQ phase can become a real problem. Quoted from the chapter: Phase-the bi-product.

We know that affecting the frequencies that we have chosen for equalization also affects the phase of those selected frequencies in relation to the unaffected frequencies. The process itself also affects the frequency response of the signal being treated. We are talking about tiny offsets here. Every time a frequency range is selected and treated, the affected frequencies will exhibit displacement in relation to the unaffected frequencies. This offset is phase.

This is particularly apt when using EQ on a sound and then layering it with the original. As displacement of the affected frequencies now exists phase will be evident. It is this phase that we hear and remark on when talking about doubled vocals as 'fatter' or 'thicker'.

If the displacements are wider apart and more distinct then phasing will be more pronounced. Depending on the type and amount of EQ applied this can be construed as chorus or distortion in very extreme cases. In this instance distortion applies as degradation of the signal. Not really something we strive for when processing vocals.

The best way of dealing with EQ on multi layers is to audition the layers in unison. One vocal line treated with EQ might sound great on its own, but when layered with the other vocal lines could sound poor or out of place. Make a habit of processing files individually but auditioning them together.

Use more than one copy of a vocal line

The best example of this, and the one I am going to start the walk through examples with, is using more than one copy of a vocal line to create depth, width and harmonies for the chorus.

Figure 13.1 is a snapshot of one vocal file, imported three times on three separate audio tracks, and treated with three separate EQ units. I have used an older version of Cubase (VST) as the imagery is cleaner and more detailed. Please apply the same settings in your host sequencer and its vsts.

I have then EQ'd each one with emphasis on the three different frequency bands; low, mid and high. I have created a 'humped' peak for the low-mid section, emphasising frequencies at around the 2.5 kHz region upwards. Additionally, the other two curves show an almost shelf like response but with very subtle compensation at each peak range. The file will sound very similar to the original file, in fact almost identical (Figure 13.1). Listen to the original file (Vocal 1 clean.wav) and then listen to the processed file (Vocal 1-3 way EQ.wav).

The reasoning is that with these three layers I am now able to conduct some subtle and extreme EQ curves. I am also able to pan the three versions and create a new texture from all three curves. There is some form to this thinking, and

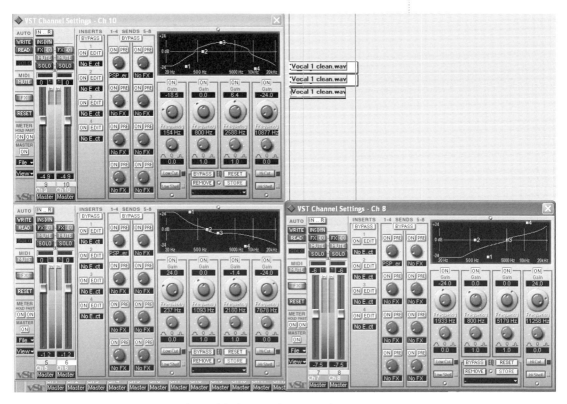

it will become clearer as we move along with the next few examples.

The reason all three files sound so close to the single original file is because I have shaped the separate frequencies such that when they are all combined (or layered), they will look and sound the same as the single original file.

Now let us look at what happens if I pan the three files to selected positions in the stereo field (Figure 13.2), and more importantly, listen to the treated file.

By panning the individual files, we are able to hear the EQ treatment far better than having all the files central. You can now compare the files, and it is clear

Figure 13.1
Vocal with three separate EQs.

Sound file

Vocal 1. 3 way EQ panned.wav

Figure 13.2
Panned version.

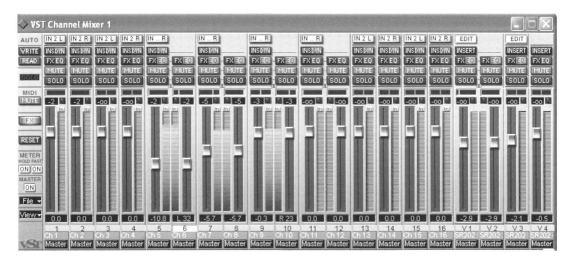

that the files that have undergone EQ and panning sound wider and deeper than the lone original file. This technique is a great way to widen those vocal tracks, and to add some depth in the process.

Making copies of the original untreated file while running the copies alongside the original and then applying different EQ curves, will afford us huge flexibility and variety. If the vocals were double or multi tracked then we would have had even more options, as the multi recorded vocals would have sounded different every time. The beauty of this simple technique is that you can alter the EQ curves and create further textures and pan positions. It is endless how many variations and textures can be achieved with simple use of EQ.

If you check the images for the vocal EQs you will see that there have also been gain changes on the masters for each individual channel. Basically, I have compensated for the extreme EQ gains by lowering the channel outputs. As mentioned earlier please take care when boosting, particularly with the extreme amounts I have used.

Knowing that EQ is about boosting or cutting frequencies will help you to go a long way in achieving better mixes, as gain compensation is one of the most crucial aspects of EQ.

Another way of performing the above would have been to do the exact opposite and cut where there have been boosts, and boost where there have been cuts. If the overall curves are peaking high in gains then it makes sense to compensate by using cutting as the first option, and then boosting around the cuts. But this is pure technique and semantics. As we are in a virtual domain, and the vsts are simply code then either process can be applied. The trick is to know where and when to compensate. As mentioned earlier there are distinct advantages to cutting, so bear that in mind when you start eating into the headroom.

Extreme EQ curves

We can take this a step further and create great effects for the vocals in our mix. Figure 13.3 shows the same vocal line being treated as before, but this time we are going to use some extreme EQ curves for the copies, and create interesting effects. What I have done here is to move two of the copies to create an interesting panned effect, Figure 13.4, (simply by moving the start points of each audio file). However, I have used extreme EQ curves for two of the copies so as to create some new and interesting sonic textures.

Figure 13.3
Extreme EQ.

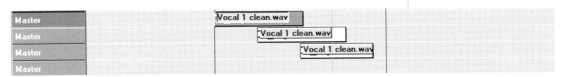

This is an example of creative EQ. It is a great feeling to be a producer today simply because the tools we have available can make for some creative effects. Feel free to reshape any of the EQ curves and listen to each outcome. This will attune your ears and teach you what works and what doesn't.

Figure 13.4
Move two of the copies to create an interesting panned effect.

Removing a frequency anomaly

The following example is one of corrective EQ. It makes sense to show you how important corrective EQ is when dealing with vocals. This is the application of Primary EQ. I have deliberately left a frequency anomaly in this audio file, just before the final vocal line, so that we can use a notch filter to remove the rogue frequency (Figures 13.5 and 13.6). Listen to the anomaly here. You can clearly hear it just before the second line comes in. I have highlighted the rogue frequency so that you can easily see where it sits.

Sound file

Vocal extreme EQ anomaly.wav

Figure 13.5
Extreme EQ anomaly.

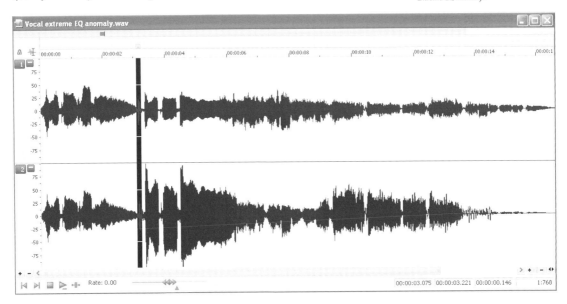

By zooming in tightly on an area, we can easily determine the nature of the problem that might lie in there. In this case we have found the anomaly and it is clearly visible.

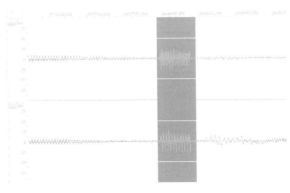

Figure 13.6
Extreme EQ anomaly (zoomed in).

Figure 13.7
Spectrum Analysis

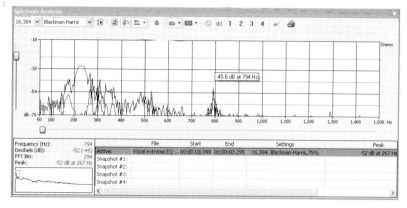

Figure 13.7 shows the use of the Spectrum Analyser in determining the frequency range of the anomaly. I have determined that the anomaly lies around the 800 Hz region, and now I will use the notch filter in the paragraphic EQ within Sound Forge to remove the anomaly. Your ears can be your best friends here. By listening to the anomaly, while adjusting the parameters on the notch filter, we can 'hear' the changes we make.

Figure 13.8
Notch Settings

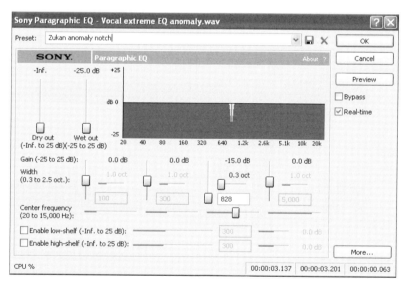

As you can see I have selected a bandwidth that encompasses enough of the anomaly without interfering too much with the sung vocal line.

When using a notch filter it is not just about the frequency selected, gains and Q values (where needed) but also about the bandwidth (discussed earlier). Try to be wary when selecting the actual width because if it is too narrow you might have small amounts of the anomaly still audible at the extremes beyond the width. The same is true in reverse; too much width and you start to eat into the frequencies of the adjoining frequencies. I have now made the changes and have rendered the process

That is what we call Corrective EQ. Any EQ unit that allows you to have detailed control over a frequency range can only be a positive tool. To fully utilise a notch fil-

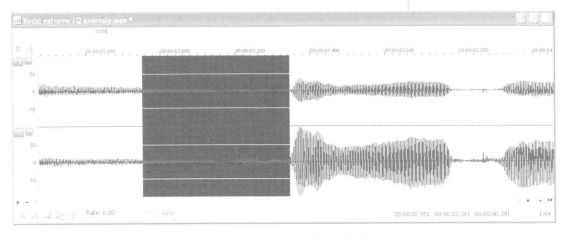

ter, we need to be able to home in on any frequency band and have the ability to remove or reduce the gain of that band. I must say, I use notch filters all the time and rate them as one of the most potent corrective tools available.

With the simple combination of using the Spectrum Analyser and the notch EQ, it is endless what you can achieve. Notch filters are also used for pops, clicks and plosives and is fact one of my 'go to' tools when dealing with Primary EQ.

Notch filters are not limited to processing vocals - they can be used for just about any type of sound, but the bandwidth is crucial when deciding which EQ to use. Some EQs have more detailed parameters and are therefore more useful for a certain type of process. In other cases a simple notch filter with basic parameters can be invaluable.

Other EQ effects

As I mentioned earlier in this book, frequency charts are only guides at best. Use the Spectrum Analyser, a decent audio editor and your ears. They are better than any chart. Here are a few more EQ curves for the types of effects that you hear quite often in commercial releases:

The nasal/telephone effect

Listen to the original untreated file (Vocal 2 clean). In terms of creating the telephone (narrow banded) effect, it is simply a case of using the right filter types with the right amount of cuts and in the right frequency range. The idea is to narrow band the frequencies (smaller resultant bandwidth) and to cut the low-end and hi-end frequencies to leave the mid-range frequencies.

For this purpose I have chosen a simple 2 node EQ, but have selected a hi-pass filter for the low-end and a low-pass filter for the high-end. This means that I am now only concentrating on the frequency range between these two limits. As discussed in Chapter 8 ('Types of EQ'), this type of filter is called a band-pass filter (basically a low-pass and hi-pass filter combined).

Figure 13.10 shows the frequency region and range I have selected, and by applying cuts I am able to home in on this range and create the narrow banded telephone effect. Please remember to compensate the gains when boosting or cutting.

Figure 13.9

Sound file

Vocal extreme EQ anomaly

Sound file

Vocal 2 clean.wav

Info

All the sound files referred to in this book can be downloaded from:

www.pc-publishing.com/soundeq.html

Figure 13.10
Telephone effect.

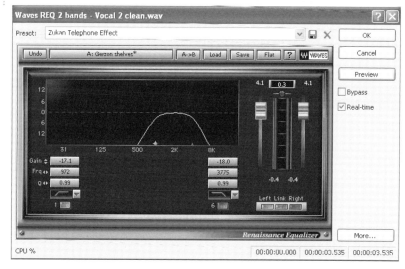

Figure 13.10
Telephone effect.

Sound file

Vocal 2 telephone effect.wav

Soft mid roll-off

This EQ curve is a gentle curve, although there are some hefty boosts at the low frequency ranges with a slight dip (cut) at the low-mid to mid, and then a slight boost in the hi-mid to high frequency ranges. This is neither corrective nor creative; it is simply a way of showing you how to shape a sound to allow for more dynamic content.

As you can hear from the original (Vocal 2 clean) file, the vocal line is a little flat with a slightly brittle attack and a pronounced mid energy. So, by compensating for the attack element and the mid and hi-ranges, I have given the vocal line a little more richness and a better overall frequency flatness. This could be regarded as Primary EQ as it is a preparation for the Secondary EQ stage mix process.

You can, of course, shape the frequency content in any way you choose, especially when layering or mixing for a specific genre and effect.

Figure 13.11
Soft mid roll-off.

Sound file

Soft mid roll-off.wav

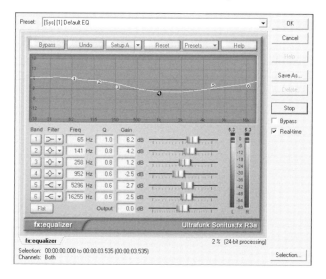

Presence

I am using the original (Vocal 1 clean) for this example as it is a brighter and more sibilant example and therefore requires a little 'manoeuvring'. Listen to the final rendered file: Vocal 1 presence.wav.

As discussed earlier the 'air' band is around the 14 kHz and above. The image shows an 8.4 dB boost around 15-16 kHz and a little 2.3 dB boost at around 2 kHz to add a little distinction in the vocal's attack and lo-mid . I selected Bell shapes as this maintains smooth peaks and gives the EQ curve a more fluid shape, with it moving smoothly from one range into another. The vocal sounds as if it has far more presence than before, with a nice and airy top-end and a pronounced attack in the lo-mid to mid-range.

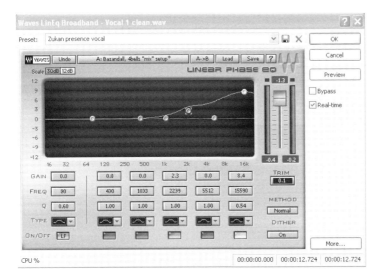

Figure 13.12
Presence.

This EQ curve can also be used for sounds that are rich in most of the frequency content and peak at the higher end. It is also good for adding presence or sparkle to mixes, but needs far more detailed analysis so as not to overdo the process.

Mixes by their very nature are played on systems whereby the higher end frequencies dissipate quicker (clubs etc) and therefore to compensate many will boost the high-end frequencies too much and the mix will then sound 'top heavy' and too bright. I often recommend the use of good semi-closed headphones to audition high frequency processing. Of course, an acoustically treated room is even better.

When boosting such high frequencies, please be very careful as to the type of material being treated. Percussive sounds can become harsh when boosted so high up the spectrum. Metallic sounds such as cymbals or hi hats can become harsh and be brought far more forward in the mix than desired.

Excessive high frequency content can quickly tire the ears, and I often consider a high boost of this nature as more of a thinning of the low mid frequencies.

And finally, to fully appreciate the 'air' band, it is necessary to audition these frequencies in an acoustically treated room with a decent frequency response, as 'felt' frequencies (as opposed to heard) can be falsely represented in a poor environment.

Sibilance taming

In this example I have used a single band with a low-pass filter selected for type. The result is that I have tamed the sibilance (the 'sss' sound) from the vocals. I did not select a lower frequency as this would have compromised most of the high-end and made the vocals sound dull. Additionally, I have steered away from using a higher frequency value so that you can hear the difference between the rendered file and the original. As with all my examples, I use slightly over the top figures so as to best display the end result.

Figure 13.13
Sibilance taming.

Sound file

Sibilance taming vocal2.wav

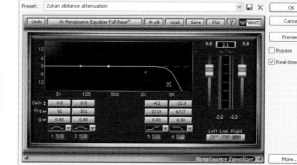

And by using the low-pass filter shape I am able to attenuate frequencies beyond the selected point. A bell would not have helped, as it would have looked more like a notch (Figure 13.14), as the bell shape would be inverted (cut) and then rise back up to the 0 line.

Figure 13.14
Bell shape.

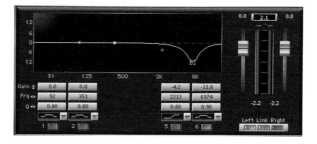

The hi-shelf can work, but offered a peak in the response with those selected values, and that didn't quite work for this example (Figure 13.15).

Figure 13.15
Hi-shelf.

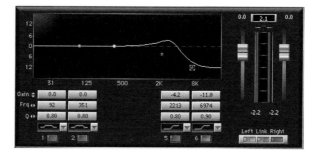

If you study the examples above, you will notice that the EQ curves that cut, as opposed to boost, have a more gentle effect on the sound, and can be quite pronounced – even with small cuts. The combination of cuts and boosts help to shape the sound in more detail, and to make the overall curve look more natural; the only exception being the 'nasal effect'. For this, we need to zoom in on a select frequency band, and treat that band in relation to all the other bands.

Filter types and bandwidth play crucial roles in defining the final curve of the response, so understanding and experimenting with these will greatly help you conquer EQ chores far more quickly and efficiently.

Whenever you create an EQ curve, name it and save it within your software plug-in. That way you have ready made templates to use when required, as with all presets they will put you in the ball park region of where and how to process.

Lead and backing vocal mix

Finally, I would like to close this chapter with a lead and backing vocal mix. If you listen to the audio file that was sent to me you will notice that there are already delays, pans, compression and some EQ present in the vocals.

I often get projects like this, where there is only the lead and backing vocals and a stereo master of the drum loop. The reason for this is that labels will often request another version of the vocals mix to use either as referencing against their existing mix or to include as another version.

In this instance I was sent the vocals and the drums. I have only included one section of the whole song so as to show you how to process an already processed file with a couple of simple procedures. The section I have chosen is a section with varying dynamics and tonal changes, and without going into some serious automation or drawing in EQ curves at varying measures of the mix, I thought it far more pertinent to concentrate on the 'difficult' section.

Figure 13.16 shows the Spectrum Analyser being used in real-time. The advantage of using the Spectrum Analyser in real-time is that you can gauge the movement of the frequencies across time while the music is playing.

As is obvious from its shape, the low frequency peaks are drum based peaks, and the ranges from around 800 Hz onwards encompass the rest of the vocals

Sound file

vocal 3 bv lead dry.wav

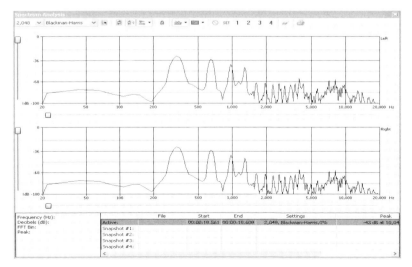

Figure 13.16
Real time Spectrum Analyser.

Info

All the sound files referred to in this book can be downloaded from:

www.pc-publishing.com/soundeq.html

along with the drums. At different parts of the vocal section this graph will change so it is very useful to keep an eye on the changes in real-time.

I have not processed these vocals in any other way bar using EQ. With dynamically sung vocals I would normally use automation to control the levels prior to any further processing. Compression would come last – this would level off any rogue peaks. However, for this example I have kept the peaks intact so you can clearly hear the frequency ranges I have boosted. Figure 13.17 shows the curves and values.

Figure 13.17
Curves and values.

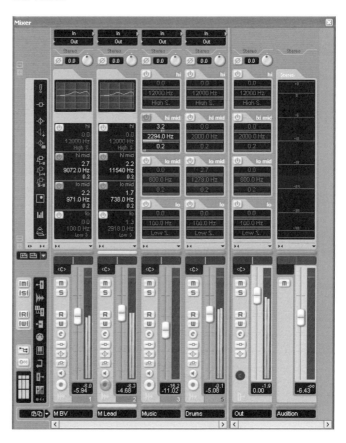

The backing vocals (BV) have been treated with a small 2.2 dB boost at 970 Hz to give them a little more presence at the low-end and to give the perception of 'warmth'. I have concentrated a boost of 2.7 dB at 9 kHz so as to give the line more mid-to-top, so as to give the perception of more body and snap.

The lead line has had a small boost of 1.7 dB at 730 Hz, just to level off the low-end in line with the BVs. This makes it sound more uniform and gels the two lines better (as opposed to hearing two distinct lines). I have also applied a small boost of 2.2 dB at 11.5 kHz to pronounce the body of the vocals a little more and to keep the range in line with the backing vocals.

Sound file

vocal 3 bv lead EQd.wav

The result of these very simple vocal line processes allows the vocals to sound fuller with no emphasis on extremes and gels them a little more into a uniform tone.

The example above is as simple as you can get, simply because the vocal frequencies, prior to any processing, were already rich in frequencies (albeit a little restricted). My job was made harder because of the delays and pans, and this can always be a problem as will be discussed in the next chapter. Sometimes all you need are very small changes to create a bigger impact. The above example fits this thinking nicely.

Please try to bear in mind that when you have applied automation to a track (to control dynamics) then the EQ curves will change too. If you bear in mind that level automation is about controlling gains, while EQ is about gain changes of specific frequency bands, then you can see why this area is an important one to understand.

Key frequencies for vocals

With vocals, there are certain frequency ranges that might be worthwhile to note, just in case you need to rely on inputting values into an EQ unit (as opposed to using nodes and 'drawing' the EQ shape). They are not Gospel, but can be helpful, particularly when dealing with vocals. So, please take the following as a guide and nothing more.

Fundamental frequencies of the vocals are crucial when dealing with 'plosives', particularly at tracking. Additionally, it is around the fundamental that boosting can create the 'boomy' effect.

- Between 3.5 kHz – 6 kHz, you will find the main 'body' of the vocal. Boosting this will add more to the low-end of the vocal line, and cutting it will place the sound further away, and also allow the sound to be thinner.
- 6.5 kHz – 12 kHz is where the 'breathiness' and sibilance of the voice resides. This is the area that can be very useful when it comes to removing anomalies or boosting the breath effect.
- 12 kHz – 20 kHz is the range that the crispness of the vocal resides in. This is the area that needs attention if you need to soften the delivery of the vocal, or boost if you need the more pronounced characteristics of the vocal. This area can carry a lot of high energy and therefore needs care when processing with EQ, as EQ affects the apparent loudness of the audio signal.

Try to continually reference the processed version of the vocal to the dry version – and in reference to shared frequencies. Vocals that sit in a frequency range shared by other sounds need processing both in isolation (when dealing with more than one vocal line) and in reference to the shared frequencies. Trying to process a mix of cluttered mid-range frequencies can be daunting, so it makes for good strategy to work from the most important frequencies outwards, i.e. vocals, followed by all the shared frequencies, and then to the extremes.

Working on more than one vocal line requires that all the vocals be grouped into their relevant spaces (BVs, lead, overdubs etc) and then processed in relation to each other. In this instance I tend to start with the lead vocals, followed by the layers and backing vocals, and then all the rest of the vocals. The lead, layers and backing vocals are the main focus of the song, and therefore need priority when processing.

These are all simply suggestions, and if you find that another technique works for you then please use that – but do bear in mind everything we've covered in this chapter, as the voice is the most crucial part of any song and needs to be the focus of any mixing chores.

Mixing EQ – preparation and guides

So we have come this far, and all that is left is to tidy up with a few of examples of how to use EQ in separating tracks for mixing, and using EQ for reshaping certain elements of a mix.

By now I hope you are comfortable with all that has been discussed in this book and that you feel confident to go just that little further. Armed with this knowledge, you should be in a position of strength and I know you will fully understand what I am going to show you in the following examples.

When it comes to EQ treatment within a mix, there are certain pointers that might help you:

Boosting frequencies is not encouraged unless a very specific effect is required

We covered the subject of phase, anomalies, overlaps (and pretty much everything else associated with boosting frequencies) but the most important aspect of boosting frequencies when mixing is that of headroom.

All DAWs will sum their channels to the stereo master, much like any analogue mixer. If you boost a single channel by a very small amount, this amount will show at the output stage. When you apply boosts across many channels, well, you can imagine what will happen; all the values will be summed at the output stage and the headroom will be eaten into.

We have discussed headroom and what it means and in the case of dynamic processing, whereby gain is an integral if not the most important aspect of the process. Boosting will eat into the headroom. And when you start using EQ on multi channels as is the norm nowadays (for some reason), then that headroom will disappear fast.

EQ is one type of dynamic processing. Now imagine what happens when another gain related dynamic process like compression is introduced. The more boosting processes that are introduced into the signal path, the more the headroom is compromised.

Generally, I always take all dynamic processing potential outcomes into account when setting up my tracks for mixing. I always accommodate the headroom and compensate at every stage, keeping an eye on the master output meters. If you have to boost then make sure it is in small amounts and with consideration for the headroom.

Cutting frequencies will dramatically improve your task of separating instruments and vocals

Taking away, in this instance, amounts to giving. We have been through this in detail. Always think ahead and do not get confined by huddling all your frequencies into a narrow range. Remember that the more range you have in your mix, the more the dynamic movement, space and depth.

No single sound should dominate. If all frequencies are correctly treated, then the listener will enjoy the mix much more, and will find something different in the tonal content every time he or she listens to it.

But strangely enough, we have a dilemma when it comes to cutting (you thought boosting was the only culprit, pah?). We end up with a low level signal and that usually leads to one result: boosting the overall gain of the mix to compensate for the weaker signal. This invariably has one outcome: the noise floor gets raised along with the signal.

Microphone

That might not sound too bad as we are already working in a digital domain and therefore expect our signals to be pristine clean. But that is not always the case; the reason for that is that most songs require vocals and maybe some acoustic instrumentation, and for these to end up in our mixes we need to record them. Enter the microphone.

Quite often I am confronted with 'noisy' recording of vocals and that usually stems from poor gain staging, poor mic selection, inadequate room conditions, vocalist's technique and delivery and so on. Hence I always have to perform Primary EQ and a host of other noise removal processing etc. The 'noise' might be extremely subtle and you would have to be a bat to hear it, but if it exists then it will be heard, by someone somewhere. This noise will be boosted along with the rest of the signal.

Personally, I make sure that all recordings are as clean as possible and have a good dynamic range. I then work in a 24/96 environment and then dither down to 16 bits and use a good SRC (sample rate converter) to down-sample to 44.1.

The 24 bits allow me a far higher dynamic range and therefore more headroom, and the higher sample rate allows for finer and more detailed processing when dealing with EQ - that amounts to a more 'analogue' type effect. Of course, this is not bible and you can easily work in 16/44.1, absolutely nothing wrong with that. But when it comes to multi EQ tasks, I use a higher sample rate; with today's hard drive spaces and CPU power being so advanced, it makes sense to work off a higher resolution.

The best advice I can give when cutting is to marry cutting and boosting together sensibly. Wild gains are not helpful, but then huge cuts aren't either. Plan your mix process in advance and try to accommodate for the dynamic processing.

Be aware that when you boost too many sounds then the tendency is to boost other sounds to bring them up on par with level. The reverse is true for cutting. Cut too many sounds and you end up either lowering the gains of all the tracks across the board to bring them on par with the level changes, or you end up increasing the noise floor when trying to compensate for a weak signal.

Try *not* to EQ the final mix

Let the mastering house take care of this as any dynamic processing is destructive. Destructive means it cannot be reversed. The mastering house will not thank you if you have squeezed the dynamic range of all the frequencies into a narrow band, or tried to perform the old and highly mistaken trick of boosting all the frequency bands in the hope of adding 'oomph' to the mix.

If you are not sending the mix to be mastered and want a certain 'colour' or 'flavour' for the mix then by all means EQ the stereo master. In fact, I have often created copies of a mix and then experimented with the copies using different EQ curves to attain a certain sound for a specific genre or medium (club mix etc). Feel free to experiment but note that the same rules apply whether you are using EQ on a single sound or an entire mix. Any dominance in a frequency band will tire the listener.

I have often come across mixes that exhibit pronounced high frequencies and this has invariably 'hurt' my ears after a while. The same applies for mixes that are too pronounced in the lower frequencies. They can get tiresome after a while. The brain needs to be kept interested, and this is usually achieved with the mix having a good dynamic range rich in frequencies across as much of the spectrum as available. The peaks and troughs in the mix, the selection of frequencies and the presentation of those frequencies in the context of the listening experience all add up to a track that does not tire or bore the listener.

Try to start your EQ tasks with sounds that occupy extremes of frequency

Bass, high strings, deep kick, hi snares etc. Once you have sorted out the extremes, you can then start to fill up the space left in between, and once this is done you can then EQ with detail to attain width, depth and separation.

It is a bit like painting. You paint the background on the canvas. You then add all the primary colours etc. And you finally finish off with the detail and shades.

The exception to this method is when there are vocals in the mix. In this instance I generally start by working around the vocal ranges. The idea is to get a clear and balanced mix of the vocals and then to apply Primary EQ for any correction and then 'fit' the music around the vocals. This is not 'set in stone' but simply advice based on how I, and many others work. As the vocals are the most important aspect of any song it makes sense to start from there and then work 'outwards' (in terms of frequencies), separating and blending the frequencies to accentuate the vocals. Once the basic vocals are in place and treated for optimum presentation then you can apply EQ to all the other sounds.

Once a basic mix is created it is then far easier to come back to each element in the mix and apply creative EQ to further shape the sonic structure. However, as with all EQ tasks, I A/B the mix continuously with each preceding mix so as to gain a clear insight into the changes made and their effect on the overall mix. With this in mind it makes perfect sense to apply small EQ changes until the overall effect is achieved.

The voice is always 'king' in any mix, so pay particular attention to the tonal qualities of the vocal lines, both in terms of frequencies and levels and also in terms of the way the vocal lines are delivered. Primary (corrective) EQ should be your first concern followed by treatment of all surrounding frequencies. You can always use creative EQ when you have a solid foundation to work from.

Do you apply EQ before or after panning?

This is a very important question and one that has a double sided answer. If the EQ process is to apply separation then it is important to think about how a sound may sound when panned. Quite often when a sound is panned it will exhibit separation simply because it has been moved away from the centre frequencies (which are usually the 'cluttered' range of frequencies). This is because so many sounds share common mid-range frequencies.

However, when the sound is panned to a location where other sounds reside then that can clutter the newly designated space. In this instance you need to ask yourself whether the EQ should be applied in context after the sound has been panned or before. If the sound is EQ'd after panning then that will influence any other sound that is moved into that area of the stereo field. Additionally, the fact that the sound has now been panned means that once EQ has been applied and the sound is moved again it will accentuate the EQ result and affect the other surrounding frequencies.

Panning has very distinct characteristics and to understand these characteristics it is essential to understand the Panning law.

Panning law

Certain things happen to a sound when it is panned from one side of the field, through the centre, and then to the other side of the field.

When you are dealing with monaural sounds you have to take into account the dynamics of the sound when it is moved and summed. This is very important when it comes to the mix stage as many people seem to complain about how the sound behaves when it is panned, to the point that most software developers have tried to accommodate for the panning law in their coding.

The problem facing most newcomers to this industry is that once a project is mixed in certain software, the pan settings change when the project is then imported in separate mix software. This is down to how software processes the panning law, compensating for the characteristics of the process.

When a signal is panned centrally, the exact same signal will be output on both the left and right audio channels. If you were to pan this signal from the extreme left channel through the centre and then onto the extreme right channel, it will sound as if the level rises as it passes through the centre. To overcome this, mixer designers engineered the panning law to introduce a 3dB level drop at the centre, relative to the edges (left and right extremes). If you were to sum the left and right channels in a mono situation, the centre gain would result in a 6dB rise, so attenuating by that amount became a must in the broadcast industry as mono compatibility is always a prime issue.

The panning law determines the relationship between the sound's apparent image position and the pan knob control. This refers to the way the sound behaves when it is moved across the stereo field. The usual requirement is that it moves smoothly and linearly across the field. This is, of course, pertinent to log/anti-log laws.

If there was a linear gain increase in one channel and a linear gain decrease in the other channel (to change the stereo position), at the centre position, the sum of the two channels sounded louder than if the signal was panned full left or full right.

This is why we had to attenuate the gain whenever we panned a sound centrally. Digital consoles and the digital domain started to change this thinking and accommodate and compensate for this behaviour. It became necessary to attenuate the centre level by four common centre attenuation figures: 0, -3. -4.5 and -6dB. The -3dB figure is the most natural because it ensures that the total acoustic power output from the studio monitors remains subjectively constant as the source is panned from one extreme of the stereo field to the other.

However, it also produces a 3dB bulge in level for central sources if the stereo output is summed to mono, and that can cause a problem for peak level metering for mono signals. So, most broadcast desks employ 6dB centre attenuation (-6dB) so that the derived mono signal is never louder than either channel of the stereo source. However, sounds panned centrally may end up sounding a little quieter than when they are panned to the edges.

The answer is to simply compromise and split the difference and this is what led to most modern analogue consoles working off a 4.5dB centre attenuation (-4.5dB).

So, what does this mean to you and how does it help you, particularly if you are working ITB (in the box) and with different software? The answer is quite simple: find out what the software panning preferences are and adjust to taste. Most of today's software will allow for fine tuning the panning law preferences; Cubase, along with most of the big players, has a preference dialogue box for exactly this. Cubase defaults to -3dB (classic equal power), but has settings for all the standards and I tend to work off -4.5dB.

If you stay with the old school days of 0 dB, then you are in 'loud centre channel land', and a little bit of gain riding will have to come into play to smooth out the gains when panning. Check your software project and make sure you set the right preference, depending on what the project entails in terms of the mix criteria.

Understanding the above will help you greatly when structuring your projects, and if you select a certain preference then take its values and behaviour into account when using EQ.

The flip side to the EQ 'before or after' panning issue is that if you EQ before you pan, you might find that you still have issues regarding clashes, masking etc - much the same as EQ after pan, simply because once panned the sounds might invade spaces in a far more pronounced manner. But there is a difference when using EQ before panning. Basically the aim is to apply separation, depth, richness etc to the frequencies in the mix, so it follows that the first step is to separate all the frequencies, share the ones that are needed (enriching frequencies) and get the general frequency balance of the mix in order. Once this has been achieved then panning will simply place sounds in their respective stereo locations. If a sound appears to need more treatment, then treating it is far simpler than first panning and then applying EQ; this unbalances the frequency mix, therefore leading you to compensate by adding even more treatment.

Panning sounds prior to treatment can give the impression that the sounds are now separated. So, it pays to think the project through before adopting either thinking. But is this the right approach? Is there a right and wrong way, and which is preferable? There are advantages and disadvantages to both and it comes down to the material being processed and the goal being aimed for. So the 'right/wrong' question doesn't really help.

My guide to myself is that I will pan sounds first just to hear what spaces are occupied and whether the mix sounds better with these panned sounds; and if further tweaking is required I will then apply the necessary processes. The reason, at least for me, is quite simple. Some mixes may sound cluttered when everything is central, but when panned the mix sounds richer and more spatial as the frequencies are now spread. This is particularly true of mixes that have very few sounds. By moving one sound away from another, space is created and filled. The additional advantage of this is that in some cases, no treatment at all is required and the original frequencies recorded stay intact.

If I decide to EQ first and then pan, I am faced with one possible problem; once a sound is separated and then moved, the impression of too much distance is achieved and 'thinning' (distance between frequencies in a mix) can take place. If you take this thinking one step further then the sage advice from seasoned producers is to 'process only when needed'. This simply means that there is no real need to alter any sound if it has been chosen and recorded as near to what was required, especially if it already sits nicely in the mix and sounds 'right'.

Panning first, and then apply EQ if needed seems to fit that premise. You might find that once the sounds are panned, EQ is not even needed.

Cleanliness is next to godliness

Keep your sounds clean. If you need to use corrective EQ to eliminate anomalies then do so, but do not boost any anomalies within the chosen frequency range.

Working from a clean slate will give you the best results. A poorly constructed sound file will play havoc with all the other sound files and make the task of mixing a nightmare. It only takes one bad sound file to ruin a mix. If there is something that cannot be easily corrected, try to get the original raw file. In the event that there is no access to the original file then re-recording could be a good option, as a clean and dynamic sound file will be a good reference for all the other sound files in the mix project. However, this is not always the case in the real world and quite often we have to make do with what we have. If this is the case then Primary EQ should be first and foremost on your agenda.

No one said 'You have to EQ'

If your sound files are already clean and dynamically strong and sit nicely in the mix, then you might find that they actually do not need any EQ treatment at all.

Purists will support the no EQ tradition. You have the luxury of choosing to EQ or not, but be aware that you do not have to EQ to attain a good mix.

Quite often, the recordings themselves will have been made in an ideal environment; correct room (and ambiances), good selection of microphones, and decent pre-amps. The same applies to clean and nicely balanced recordings of any instrument. Synthetic sounds can also fall into the 'no EQ required' department so long as the correct sounds with the right frequency content have been selected. But to be honest, I have rarely come across a mix that does not require some form of EQ treatment. What is important is the following:

'Try not to record (track) your sounds with EQ already applied, as almost all dynamic processes are destructive, i.e. they cannot be reversed accurately, unless it is for corrective treatment. You can always apply EQ later.'

That does not mean do not use EQ. It means try to be sensible when using

EQ at the tracking stage. In some cases EQ at the recording stage might be needed (poor room or mic compensation etc). But if you have to use it then use it sensibly and in small amounts.

The following chapter will deal with certain mix examples and will concentrate on instrumental sounds as opposed to vocals, as vocals have already been covered in depth.

Mixing EQ examples – instruments

A simple mix

Let us start with a nice simple mix example. Figure 15.1 shows a very basic mix of kick, clap and a synthesizer keyboard hook. I have kept these sounds quite simple with the keyboard hook enveloping some of the higher frequencies of the kick and the mid frequencies of the clap. The dry mix sounds ok as it is, but because there is a deep and strong low-end kick the elements need some simple EQ to afford some separation and no frequency clashes.

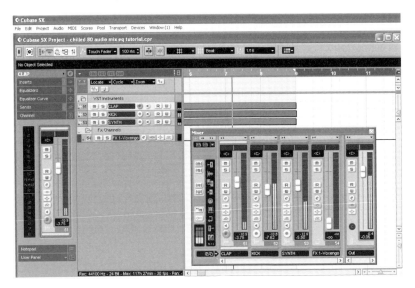

Figure 15.1
Basic mix set up

Sound file

chilled dry.wav

Listen to the dry mix. As you can see I have left ample headroom to allow for any boosts that might take place when I EQ. If you were to open the file in an audio editor it would show the audio peaking at -5 dB. I have included the image as well so as to accustom you to 'correct' procedures. Grouping the sound elements and naming them accordingly makes life a lot simpler, particularly if we then decide to send these sounds to a group for further processing.

Everyone has their own system to use but I thought if I shared mine with you it might help you understand that mixing is about structure. You will also note that in both the main arrange window and the mixer window I have 'hidden channels'. This really helps me to keep everything in view without having to go searching for active channels.

Info

All the sound files referred to in this book can be downloaded from:

www.pc-publishing.com/soundeq.html

What I am going to do now is to show you two variations of the same track. With the first version (Figure 15.2) I have given a distinct peaked boost to the kick at around 70 Hz, using a Q factor of 3.3. This has made the kick more resonant and given it a nice rounded and tight feel. If I was only interested in gentle curves with no distinction around a frequency then I would have left the Q value at below 1, in fact probably untouched.

With the clap I have boosted around the 2 kHz to bring out a little more snap and crunch into the sound. To accommodate the kick's new found frequency I have 'topped' (applied top-end boost to) the synth line at around the 5 kHz range. The three together have given a new colour and flavour to the simple track. This is an instance of creative EQ.

Figure 15.2

The curves and values for all three channels

Sound file

Chilled eq curves 1.wav

If you were to open the file in an audio editor you would see that the headroom has been eaten into with a max peak of -2 dB. Even with the EQ boosts, I have been careful to compensate via the channel gain faders for any drastic peaks and thus kept everything within the headroom.

The next mix (Figure 15.3) is far more emphasised at the low to low mid-ranges, with the kick having a low-pass shelf filter gradually decreasing towards the 2 kHz range. I did this so as to maintain the low-end of the kick with a heavy boost and then to allow the higher frequencies to get attenuated along the curve. This has allowed for far deeper and wider frequency content than the example above (which used a specified peak boost with a high Q value).

The clap has actually had a cut applied at around 60 Hz. Although you may think that this is strange (as you do not expect a clap sound to enter this low range) it might surprise you to know how many clap and snare sounds possess low-end frequencies. By cutting this range I am allowing both the kick and synth line to explore this range uncoloured.

Finally, I have boosted the synth line at around 1.4 kHz to emphasise the body and tail off of the attack.

If you look at the three EQ curves and try to visualise one on top of the other, you will see how much low to mid boosts exist, and this has been emphasised more by the cutting of the low-end from the clap. This new mix sounds thicker and fuller and encompasses far more of the lower and mid frequencies than the mix previously. The file peaks at -1 dB when opened in an audio editor.

What I have tried to show with these two simple examples is how easy it is to shape frequencies without having to resort to extreme processing measures. The combination of boosts and cuts also allows for a smoother final curve with less compensatory measures having to be taken to tame to gains.

Add more elements

Figure 15.4 is an example containing more musical elements and I chose this particular track because of all the shared frequencies.

As you can hear, this mix is both bass heavy and snare biased. The synth line and piano are interfering with each other as they are sharing frequencies. The kick is meant to be a tight rolling kick, created to give a 'moving along' feel to the track as opposed to a 'in your face' type of low-end dominant kick.

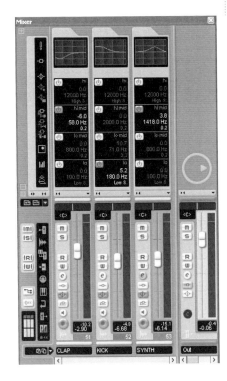

Figure 15.3
The new EQ curve

Sound file

Chilled eq curves 2.wav

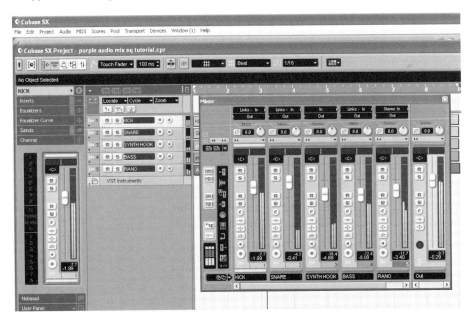

Figure 15.4
More musical elements

Although there are only five musical elements in this track the mix sounds quite full but not defined. Of course, the sounds not being panned clutter the mix somewhat, especially down the middle ranges. The goal here is to find a decent balance between all the frequency ranges and apply separation. What is most crucial here

Figure 15.5
Solos selected for the drums and bass

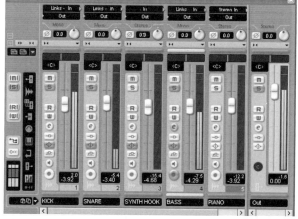

Sound file

purple dry.wav

is the 'effect' that is being sought. Is the mix intended simply for easy listening, is it meant to be genre dependent? Is it aimed at a certain medium like a club and so on? These questions always need to be asked when mixing. But general rule of thumb is to get a decent mix that exhibits good balance and separation intended for play back on all mediums. Once you have accomplished this then customising and adapting to any medium or genre will become much easier.

With this kind of a mix the most important areas to treat are the low to mid frequencies, as the 'drive' element of this track is governed by the drums and bass. The synth and piano lines are simply the overlying melodies. Once these frequency ranges are sorted out then the rest can sit nicely in and around those frequencies.

Figure 15.6
Resultant drums and bass EQ curves

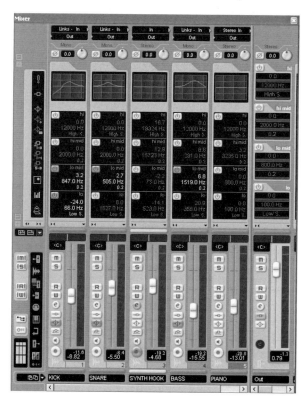

When treating drums and bass, it is always good practice to solo all these sounds (Figure 15.5) so as to continually reference each against the other both in terms of frequency management and gains/pans. I have soloed the kick, snare and bass and have treated all three together. If you listen to the sound file you will notice a nice balance and frequency spread of those three elements.

The kick has a huge 24 dB cut (low shelf) at around 66 Hz so as to remove the low-end energy and leave room for the bass to breathe in. It also has a 3.2 dB boost at around 847 Hz to give some more depth around the high-low and low-mid. The snare has a gentle 2.7 dB peak boost at around 500 Hz so as to emphasise the body more; this helps it dominate the high-end frequencies. The bass has been boosted by 6.8 dB at around 1.5 kHz due to the fact that the original source sound was a little flat and too resonant around the high mid-range frequencies, as well as being a little boomy at the low-end. I have compensated and reshaped the bass to occupy the space between the kick and snare, paying attention to enrich the low-end frequencies by layering the EQ curves. Figure 15.6 shows the resultant drums and bass EQ curves.

The next most obvious sound to EQ is the synth line; this encompasses the high-low, mid and high frequencies. This particular piano line resides mainly in the mid to high-end frequencies, so is best left to last.

The next step is to EQ the synth line with the drums and bass. And finally the piano can be treated. This is usually the order I follow. I group all the relevant frequency groups together such as drums and bass (low energy frequencies) and then introduce solitary ranges into the mix and compensate to taste (Figure 15.7).

Sound file

purple drum and bass solos.wav

Info

All the sound files referred to in this book can be downloaded from:

www.pc-publishing.com/soundeq.html

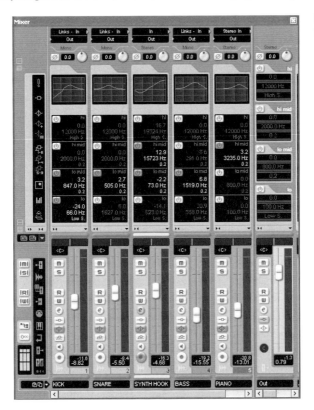

Figure 15.7
EQ curves for all the sounds

Sound file

purple all mix.wav

The most dramatic treatment has taken place on the synth line. The reason for this is that the piano, snare and the top-end of the bass occupy a lot of mid frequencies and the synth line encompasses a broad range of frequencies from high-low to high. By reshaping the frequencies with a cut at 70 Hz and a large boost at 15 kHz I have allowed the other sounds to 'breathe'.

The above is the final mix. If you open this file in an audio editor you will see that the peak value does not exceed -1.8 dB. Normally I would leave between 3-5 dB of headroom to allow for further processing (compression, further EQ, mastering etc).

A percussive beat

Finally, we are going to work on a short beat that is more percussive than instrument based. There is a huge kick, a small crunchy clap, a lead line, a bass and some panned skins (bongos, congas etc). The emphasis on the example is to blend the drum elements into a cohesive yet powerful mix.

Figure 15.8
EQ curves created for all the drum elements

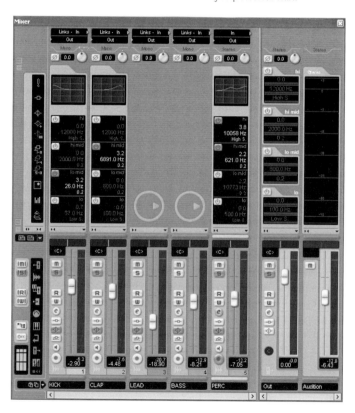

Sound file

sweet beat dry.wav

Listen to the dry version – sweet beat dry.wav. I will start by soloing the drum elements together and then working on each sound to fill the sparse spectrum. The kick is nice and big with a deep resonance. The clap is a little flat but crunchy enough to work with. The skins are nicely panned with emphasis on the low mid to mid frequencies.

The kick has been boosted by 3.2 dB at 26 Hz to provide some really low-end wooliness; for this beat, it fits perfectly. However, in most cases I would rarely boost this region, but the effect is clearly evident and works.

The clap has been boosted by 3.2 dB at around 6.8 kHz. This has added and emphasised the mid and hi-mid-range, a region where this particular clap possesses most of its body. The skins have had a double boost, one of 2.2 dB at 628 Hz (which has given some real high low-end to them) and one of 3.8 dB at around 10 kHz to give a real kick for the top-end (so as to separate the frequencies and add range). As always, I have allowed ample headroom (4.4 dB) for further processing.

To work on the bass sound I soloed the drums and the bass so as to be able to distinguish frequency crossovers, clashes and masks. I have adopted the same thinking as before, working outwards from the most dominant frequencies.

As the final image (Figure 15.9) shows I have applied a huge boost of 6.8 dB at around 500 Hz to give the bass sound more bite and low-end, and another boost of 5.2 dB at 11.5 kHz to give it a lot of top-end and separate it from the surrounding frequencies.

Sound file

sweet beat drum elements.wav

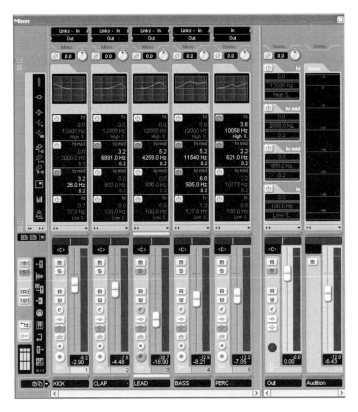

Figure 15.9
EQ Curves

Sound file

sweet beat all mix.wav

The lead line has had a simple boost of 5.2 dB at 4.2 kHz to give more body and accent this range away from the higher end, as the original lead sound was a little too bright.

The file still allows for over 4 dB of headroom and is very emphasised towards the drum and percussive elements, with the bass tucked in under the kick and the lead line kept to its lowest possible level. This allows further sounds and vocals to be added at a later date. The ample headroom is kept for reasons pointed out earlier – further dynamic processing and mastering.

Info

All the sound files referred to in this book can be downloaded from:

www.pc-publishing.com/soundeq.html

All the examples in this chapter can be bettered once effects (reverb, chorus, delay etc) and further dynamics (compression etc) are used. However, the point of these tutorials is to help you to gain an understanding of how to use EQ and the effect it can have within a mix context.

When processing a mix, try to plan out a coherent strategy. Generally and as a rule I always start with the mid-range frequencies and work outwards. Of course, this can change depending on the content of the mix and the medium it is aimed for.

Tip

Think the process through.
Compensate for the processing.
Reference against the dry mix.

- If the mix has little vocals and is very Dance orientated then think of processing the dominant frequencies, which are invariably the low to mid-range frequencies.
- If the mix is more mainstream orientated with vocals, then the mid-range frequencies need processing first, followed by the extremes or 'peripheral' frequencies.
- If the mix is very vocal orientated and sparse with instrumentation (as some R&B tracks are) then work on the vocals first and then the 'sparse' frequencies so as to add depth, width and overall 'fullness'. I could go on and on but I think you understand what I am saying.

Those three short sentences are the best advice I can give you to sum up all that has been covered in this book.

I would like to end this book with the final chapter devoted to some suggestions as to what tools I recommend when processing with EQ. These are purely subjective to me and my own personal recommendations.

Recommended tools

The Spectrum Analyser can be a great tool, but do not live by it. As we have seen already, gauging frequency detail can be very useful, but to rely entirely on the analyser's readout can be a mistake. Use your ears and the tools at your disposal, but always reference with your ears. Just because it looks good, does not mean it sounds good. But there are tools that can be of additional help and here are ones that I really like:

Harbal's Intuit Q not only acts as a great referencing tool (it can 'lift' eq curves off recorded material and allow the user to define it and use it on their own material) but it is a great educational tool as well. It offers pre-defined templates that can help the user in understanding how to apply a process. It can treat problematic frequencies, act as a frequency analyser and offers all the usual editing tools you would expect from a tool of this nature. It offers good graphical representation of 'before and after' processes (which is always helpful) and it has some nice little additional tools that can help to further shape and enhance the signal.

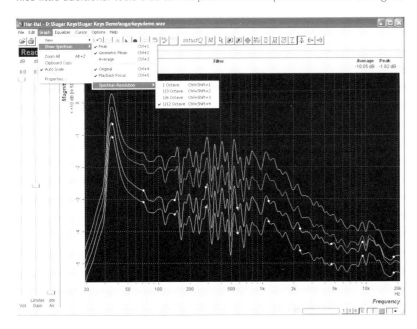

Figure 16.1
Harbal Intuit Q

Figure 16.2
Sound Forge Sonogram

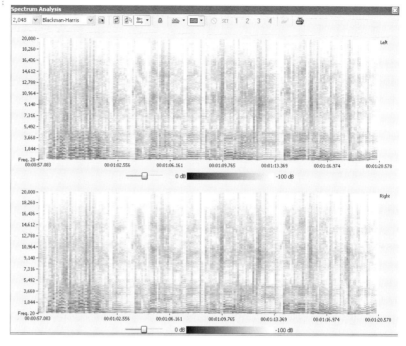

I generally use whatever process comes with the audio editor I am using at the time. I find that Sound Forge has a good array of tools for multi processing. Apart from its Spectrum Analyser it also has the facility to convert the analyser into a sonogram where the amplitude of each frequency is displayed in terms of colour (or black and white).

A good tool for showing real-time frequency analysis is Waves Paz Frequency.

Figure 16.3
Waves Paz Frequency

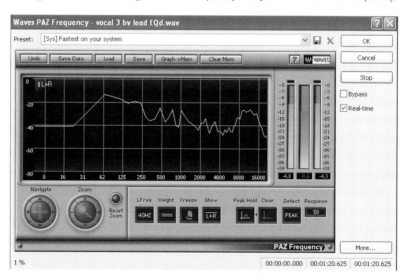

The Eiosys AirEQ is an EQ unit I really like mainly for higher end frequency management.

Figure 16.4
Eiosys AirEQ

PSP Neon is another I really like as it is transparent yet musical.

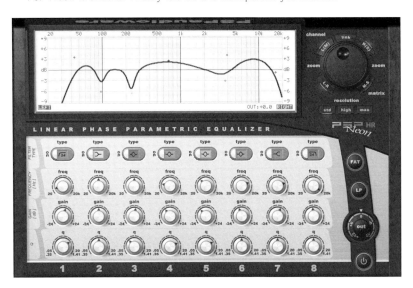

Figure 16.5
PSP Neon

PSP MasterQ is another.

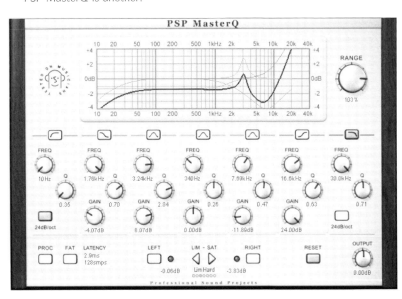

Figure 16.6
PSP MasterQ

Sonalksis sv517 mk2 is lovely and sounds very musical.

Figure 16.7
Sonalksis sv517 mk2

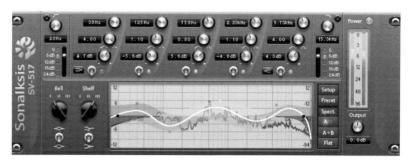

There are many more useful and highly recommended tools available and it all comes down to personal taste. Of all the tools and nice and affordable EQs recommended above, Harbal stands tall for me simply because it has so many inherent tools that are invaluable, but also because it is geared towards helping beginners (as well as helping professionals) understand the basic principles of what to look for and execute when it comes to EQ processing and, to be honest, covers far more than just EQ.

In terms of using software EQ, I must confess to preferring my hardware EQs simply because they are more musical and far better at creative than corrective EQ. Where software excels in is the corrective department and transparency. With this in mind I always use a combination of the two depending on the goals aimed for. Until coders can emulate hardware truthfully and emulate circuitry I will stick to my hybrid set up.

Final word

Well, I hope that this book has been of help to you.

I think that all the relevant and rudimentary areas have been covered, and with the addition of audio and visual examples I hope the information has come across in a simple yet detailed manner.

As with all tools, they are there to be used and experimented with. Of course, there are certain criteria that are essential and they are predominantly maths and physics related, but if you can find a balance between the two then you will be in a far stronger position to apply EQ than if you excelled in either.

Although every chapter has been subject specific and no particular subject area should be ignored, the one area that is the most crucial is that of understanding sound, how it travels and how to listen. If you cannot truthfully 'hear' what is there then how can you treat it correctly?

Until my next book, may the dynamics be with you.

Eddie Bazil (Zukan)
Samplecraze
http://www.samplecraze.com

Index